Desert and Plain, the Mountains and the River

Desert and Plain, the Mountains and the River

A Celebration of Rural America

By Berton Roueché and David Plowden

E. P. Dutton & Co., Inc. | New York | 1975

Published simultaneously in Canada by Clarke, Irwin & Company Limited, Toronto and Vancouver
ISBN: 0-525-09010-X
Library of Congress Catalog Card Number: 75-835

Library of Congress Cataloging in Publication Data
Roueché, Berton.
    Desert and plain, the mountains and the river.
    Roueché's stories were previously published in the
New Yorker between 1971 and 1973.
    1. United States—Description and travel—1960-
2. Country life—United States.   3. Roueché, Berton.
I. Plowden, David.   II. Title.
E169.02.R67   1975   917.3'04'924   75-835
ISBN 0-525-09010-X

All of the selections included in this book were previously published in their entirety in *The New Yorker*: "A Peaceable Town," December 30, 1970; "The River World," February 23, 1972; "Forty Flights of Steps," July 11, 1973; "The Grower's Shadow," August 29, 1973.

Contents

Introduction

This book is a collaboration in counterpoint. It describes —in my words and in David Plowden's photographs—an unhurried journey and three leisurely sojourns in an America that has become more foreign to many Americans than Portugal or Greece. Our collaboration is something of an experiment. Plowden and I are equal but independent partners. My reportage is not intended to explain Plowden's photographs, and his photographs are not intended to illustrate my words. We visited many of the same places, but we traveled and sojourned separately, and we offer here our separate and different depictions.

Our collaboration came about more or less by chance.

The journey I describe ("The River World") was a trip by towboat from Kansas City on the Missouri River to Baton Rouge on the Mississippi. One of the sojourns ("The Grower's Shadow") was among the farms and orchards in the high desert country of southwestern Idaho. The other visits were to small towns—to Welch ("Forty Flights of Steps"), in the mountains of southern West Virginia, and to Stapleton ("A Peaceable Town"), in the rolling grasslands of western Nebraska. These stories about an America many of us don't know, or take for granted, were published in *The New Yorker* at intervals between 1970 and 1973. Plowden read them and liked them. They also excited in him an interest to extend his own knowledge of rural America, and to record his vision of those sights. Our book began with his travels. Because certain scenes and moods are better interpreted in words, others in pictures, our stories don't necessarily overlap. Each, though, is a statement about heartland America.

My writing about America also came about more or less by chance. My visit to Welch, as noted in "Forty Flights of Steps," was entirely fortuitous. So, pretty much, was the visit described in "The Grower's Shadow." It had its inception in a remark by a Washington friend in the United States Department of Agriculture that the once ubiquitous family farm, though all but vanquished by the mammoth technologies of the factory farm, still survived and flourished in the blue distance of Canyon County, Idaho. Stapleton is another survival. It is a village self-contained and entire that has, for the moment, escaped the death grip of megalopolis. I first saw it, as have millions of other travelers, at night, from six or seven miles above the earth, from the window of an airliner—a tiny cross of pinpoint lights in an immensity of dark. It was a lonely but (to me) an appealing sight, and I took the trouble to find it and live there for a time. These visits all were made for the pleasure of discovery, or rediscovery. My river journey was undertaken for an even purer pleasure. I was born and raised in Kansas City, on the bluffs above the Missouri, and I lived and worked for several years in St. Louis, with an almost daily view of the Mississippi, but I had never more than seen these rivers. When I learned, again in the course of a casual conversation, that it was sometimes possible to arrange a passage on a towboat, I didn't hesitate.

Berton Roueché

August 1974
Amagansett
Long Island, N.Y.

The River World

The *Lesta K.*, a square-nosed, diesel-powered towboat owned and operated by the Port City Barge Line, of Greenville, Mississippi, is pushing slowly down the Missouri River toward St. Louis behind a tow of big red hopper barges loaded with Nebraska wheat and Kansas flour. There are eight barges in the tow—each riding nine feet deep in the water under fifteen hundred tons of cargo—and they are lashed two abreast. They form a raft-like mass just about seventy feet wide and almost eight hundred feet long. At the head of the tow, where I am sitting on a coil of rigging near the bow of the starboard barge, there is the feel of a raft—a peaceful sense of drifting, a sense of country quiet. The only sound is the slap of water under the rake of the bow. I am alone and half asleep in the silence and the warmth of the mild mid-morning sun. The river is empty. There is only the bend ahead and the bend behind, a sandy shore of brush and willows on the near bank, and a steep bluff crowned with cottonwoods a quarter of a mile away on the other—no towns, no houses, no bridges, no roads, not even another boat. Early this morning, after a night tied up in fog at Kansas City, we passed the mouth of the Big Blue River (originally La Rivière de l'Eau Bleue), where, one June day in 1804, the expedition headed by Meriwether Lewis and William Clark "saw a number of parroquets (*Conurus carolinensis*), and killed some deer." There are no longer any parakeets along the Missouri River (or anywhere else in America), but its shores still look as wild as they were at the turn of the eighteenth century.

I was going to St. Louis, to Cairo, to Memphis, to Natchez, to Baton Rouge, to New Orleans—I was going down the river as far as I could go. I was going as far as I could find a towboat to carry me. The packet boat has vanished from America. It has gone the way the passenger train is going. It was too slow, too comfortable, too restful. But freight still moves on the rivers. The volume, in fact, increases every year. And one can sometimes arrange for accommodations on a towboat.

I had arranged to meet the *Lesta K.* at a grain-and-molasses dock some twenty river miles above Kansas City. That was late yesterday afternoon. A friend drove me out from the city, and I was waiting on the dock when the *Lesta K.* and its thrusting tow came into view, sliding downstream on a long crossing where the channel switched from one bank to the other. The *Lesta K.* was built in 1942, but its lines are still the standard lines for towboats on the rivers. I watched it lift into sight. First, a high white pilothouse with a narrow open bridge all around and a complex of whistles and fog bells and searchlights and radio and radar antennas on the roof above. Then an open texas deck. Then the boiler deck, with a small cluster of cabins forward and two faintly fuming smokestacks aft. Then the main deck, running the length of the boat (about a hundred and fifty feet), with a deckhouse almost as long. The main deck was just above water level—there was hardly three feet of freeboard— with two tall, bumper-like towing knees at the bow. The

whistle blew. I waved. A deckhand with long, sandy hair and a horseshoe mustache waved back. He wore a T-shirt with a peace symbol on the front. The *Lesta K.* nudged gently against the dock.

The deckhand gave me a hand aboard and took me up to a cabin on the boiler deck. Behind the ferocious mask of hair and mustache was a smiling, boyish face. And he wasn't a deckhand; he was the second mate, and his name was Johnny Avent. My cabin was at the bow, just under the pilothouse, and the roar of the engines was only a distant hum. There was a single bed, a chest of drawers, a chair and a desk, a *Playboy* calendar on the wall. An inner door opened on a bathroom with a sign above the washbasin: "Potable Water." I left my bag and followed Avent down and aft to the galley. It was six o'clock, and supper was just over. Supper is at five-thirty on the river. (So is breakfast, and dinner is at eleven-thirty.) We passed the last of the five-man forward watch—the six-to-noon and six-to-midnight watch—coming along the passage. None of them looked much older than the second mate. The remains of supper were still on the table: a platter with one surviving breaded veal cutlet; dishes of peas and carrots, lima beans, green beans, creamed corn, boiled cabbage, mashed potatoes, potato chips, chili con carne, cottage cheese, and combination salad; three big biscuits on a tray; half a poundcake; a bowl of whipped cream, a bowl of canned peaches; a pitcher of iced tea, a pitcher of Kool-Aid. The cook brought me a plate and a glass of ice. He was a big man with a pale, worried face, and his name was Malone—H. L. Malone. "Or maybe you'd rather have coffee?" he said. I said I preferred iced tea. He nodded. "Yeah," he said. "Real fine." He sat down at the head of the table and gazed at a notice framed on the wall: "Pilot Rules for the Western Rivers & the Red River of the North." He frowned.

"They drink a lot of coffee on the river," he said. "Yeah —and the farther south, the more they drink. Now, I'm from Mississippi myself, but I give it up. I stopped last March, and I'll tell you something: no more heartburn. It cured it just like that. The same doctor told me to try corn oil for frying. He said it was a whole lot better. So I don't fry nothing no more in hog lard. Yeah—and another thing I learned. This was when I had me a little drive-in down home in Lexington. I used to sell a lot of pickled hard-boiled eggs. I sold dozens of them every week. But you know how hard a boiled egg is to shell. I spent half my time just peeling them eggs. Then the farmer I was buy-ing from he give me a tip. Pip them, he said. Punch a little dent in one end before you cook them. And, sure enough, they peel just like a banana. But I don't grudge the fellas their coffee. I know they like it when they go on watch, and they like it when they come off watch, and they also like it in between. So I've always got a big pot on the stove. They don't allow no liquor on the river. That's the company rule. And no gambling, either. Coffee gives the fellas something to do. The only other thing is eating. The way it works, a fella works for thirty days straight and then he's off for fifteen days, and I try to keep them happy when they're on the boat. You know what they say: a full stomach makes a patient man. There's ten of us on this boat. There's the captain and his relief. There's the chief engineer and his relief. The rest are crew and me. I will say the company understands about food. They know it's important, and they allow me around a thousand dollars a month to work with. You wait till tomorrow. Saturday dinner is the high point of the week on the river. Steak—T-bone steak, with mushrooms. All you want. I broil a couple of dozen. I fry my chicken and my pork chops and my catfish, but I broil my steak. I've been on the river for nine years—seven with Port City—and I've got my own way of doing things. I like it on the river. Of course, I don't have my wife anymore. She left me—after seventeen years of marriage. I don't think it was the river. These days, I could sleep in the morning till maybe four-fifteen, but I like to get up around three. I don't like to go right to work. I like to set around and drink tea and wake up good. I take my tea and go out on deck and set there. I like the dark and the smell of the river. And I don't let nothing bother me."

I climbed two flights of almost vertical stairs to the aerie of the pilothouse. The stairs were dark, and the pilothouse was dim with dusk and cigarette smoke. Jene Bills, the captain, was sitting there alone in the twilight at a console of levers and grips and gears and meters—a square-built man of about forty-five with smooth brown hair and a broken nose. His chair was a big leather arm-chair as high as a shoeshine chair, and it gave him a commanding view through the windows all around. I cleared away a pile of charts and magazines and sat down on a high wooden bench. The river spreading out ahead had a coppery sunset glitter. Bills craned his neck and grunted. "A lot of pilots cuss this time of day," he said. "I mean this doggone glare. But fog is worse. We've got radar—the screen is that box standing over there. We couldn't run at night without it. But radar ain't enough in fog—not on this river. The Missouri is too fast and too narrow, and the bends are too short. It's got a lot of bends that ain't but two miles long. You've got to do a lot of holding back—what we call backing up. I know a lot of pilots on the Lower River—on the Mississippi on down from Cairo—that are scared shirtless on this river. I've got a good feeling for it, but I will admit it can be trouble. It can be real hard work to go down. When you're moving along at eight or nine or even ten miles an hour and there isn't too much water in the channel, anything can happen. Like finding a bar built up on a crossing that wasn't there before. The most important tool we've got is the swing indicator. It's like a gyrocompass. It tells me if the tow is swinging out of line. It's a whole lot faster than my eye. I watch that machine as much as I watch the river. But the river is getting better, too. The Army Engineers have done a lot to stabilize the banks and maintain a decent channel. This channel used to change a couple of times a day. And the Coast Guard keeps the channel marked with buoys—like that red nun off to port. But this is still the trickiest river in the U.S.A. Coming up, it don't matter.

You're poking along at three or four miles an hour. There's nothing much for the pilot to do but set back and read his Western magazine. No close work, and plenty of time to act if need be. I mean, when you cut your engines, the current is as good as a brake. But, going down, you can stub your toe pretty easy. When your tow is put together right, when you've secured your barges end to end and side to side and the stern of the tow is fast to the tow knees—when you've done all that, why, it's just like one big boat, and it steers like one. It don't act or feel much different. But you've got to remember one thing. It's one hell of a big old boat. You can't stop it or turn it like you would your car. Not unless you want to bust it up."

The sunset glare was fading from the river. The shadows deepened along the banks. Then the last of the light was suddenly gone, and the river was only a stir of paler dark. Three little running lights appeared on the faraway head of the tow. Bills turned on a searchlight. The beam reached out across the tow through a turmoil of white willow flies. It touched a bobbing black can buoy, then a ghostly finger of sandy shoal, then a bright green jungle wall of trees. It felt back across the water and pounced on another buoy. "Another thing about this river," Bills said. "I think it's probably the cleanest. Up at Sioux City and all the way down to Omaha, it's as clear and blue as a lake. It's the prettiest, too. I guess I've been on most. The Upper Mississippi and the Lower. The Ohio. The Illinois. The Tennessee. If you want to know the truth, I've been on the river all of my life. I was born on a houseboat down at Memphis. And I guess you could say that the river was my salvation. I never had a father. I only had a stepfather, and when my mother left us, he raised me. He worked as a steeplejack when he worked. I done the rest—the cooking, the washing, the housekeeping, the woodchopping. That man never let up. He treated me worse than the meanest man would treat the sorriest dog. When I reached sixteen, I dropped out of school and run off down the river. I started out where everybody starts on the river—as a deckhand. That's the school for the river. There ain't no other. You learn to be a pilot by learning the river and watching the pilot work. Johnny Avent, the boy that brought you aboard, I'm teaching him right now. When you've made ten round trips on your river and can draw a map of its course and put in every bend by name and every light and every crossing, then you can take the Coast Guard examination. If you pass, you're a licensed pilot on that river. That's what I done. Those were still the steamboat days. I remember that long, lonesome whistle on those old steamers. It was a beautiful sound coming across the water. It was sad, but it made you feel good. There wasn't much else in those days that you'd want to brag about. Everything was different then. The river was just about the bottom of the gutter. Hell, it *was* the bottom. If you worked on the river, you were trash. People would walk away from you. But it gets you, the river. I had it in me too deep to let me quit, and I got my first license in 1950. Then things began to change. Business got better, and the pay and everything else got better, and they started crying for pilots. There still aren't near enough for the need. Last year, more than fifteen per cent of all the freight that moved in this country was carried by barge, and it's going to be more this year. The reason is the rates are so low—three mills per ton-mile. The railroads, for example, charge the shipper fifteen. There's a lot of new people coming on the river now. We're even getting college men—fellas like Johnny. They're ambitious to learn and advance. Of course, we get the other kind, too. I mean that new kind of kid they've got these days. They don't know nothing, and they don't want to learn. They don't want to work. All they want is easy living. Eat, sleep, and make a payday. Then they're long gone. And do you know the pay a deckhand gets now? Twenty-two fifty a day. That's almost seven hundred dollars for the thirty days. And no expenses—no room, no board, no nothing. They make me sick. We call this here a bulkhead and we call what we're standing on a deck. They can't be bothered. They call it walls and floor. They call the bow the front end and the head the bathroom and the galley the kitchen. And they're not all kids. Some of them are grown men. I had a mate a while back who kept talking about the capsule. I asked him what the hell was that. He said, 'Why, that thing there.' And he pointed to the capstan."

Bills reached across the console and picked up a microphone. He pressed a switch. "Johnny?" he said, and his voice splintered out from a speaker on the bridge. "Polka Dots? One of you fellas. The captain wants some coffee."

He glanced at me, but I shook my head and he put the microphone back. "Coffee gets to be a habit on the river," he said. "I seem to need it even when I'm relaxed at home. I sometimes wake up in the night and go out to the kitchen and make myself a cup. It drives my wife about crazy. But now I'm going to show you something pretty. We're coming into Kansas City. It's just around this bend, and, lighted up at night, it's the prettiest skyline on the river. I've seen them all, and nothing else can touch it."

We picked our way through a crossing and into a tight hairpin bend. There was a glow above the riverside woods ahead. We came out of the bend, and there it was—an explosion of lights, mirrored in the dark of the river and diffused across the sky, climbing steeply up a terraced bluff to a soaring summit of flashing signs and floodlit towers. I looked up at Kansas City and thought of *Huckleberry Finn:* "The fifth night we passed St. Louis, and it was like the whole world lit up." So was Kansas City.

A voice from the pilothouse speaker called me back to the boat from my front seat at the head of the tow. It was eleven-thirty and time for dinner. I walked back along the barges through a spillage history of past and present cargoes—wheat, rock salt, soybeans, phosphate rock, corn. I ate my T-bone steak (and five vegetables, baked potato, green salad, hot biscuits, vanilla ice cream) with the forward watch. They were Bills, Johnny Avent, the chief engineer, and two young deckhands—the one called Polka Dots, because he wore a red-and-white polka-dot cap, and another called Tear Drops, because soon after he came aboard the *Lesta K.* he received a shattering "Dear John" letter. Just beyond the windows at the end of the table, a long green shore of willows drifted serenely by. It was practically in the room. We sat at the table until well past noon. There was a somnolent feeling of Sunday. Afternoon is often an idle time on the river. The forward watch goes off to bed for its second installment of sleep. "What I like to do," Bills said as he pushed back his chair, "is get into bed with a good Luke Short or Frank O'Rourke or one of those, and the next thing I know, they're knocking on the door to get me up for supper." With nothing much to do, the after watch lie around on deck and smoke and talk and turn the pages of *Playboy* and *Cavalier* and *Penthouse.* Only the pilot—the relief captain—is fully awake and at work. Even the cook goes off to his room for a nap.

The pilot on the *Lesta K.* was a man named David Evans. He was a handsome, red-faced man of about thirty-five with long gray hair and with a heart tattooed on his thumb. When I came into the pilothouse, he was staring out at the river and whistling some tuneless tune. He had a mug of coffee on the console beside him, and a textbook—*The Hive and the Honey Bee.* "Beekeeping is one of my hobbies," he said. "It's an interest. I got three hundred hives down home in Mississippi—down in Choctaw County. I get a good hundred pounds of sweet-clover honey per hive. But there's so much poison in the fields these days you can't let your bees stray. You got to keep them close to home. The way you do that is plant good nectar sources nearby. The next thing I think I'll do is get me a herd of Black Angus cattle. And I want to build me a nice big home—a fifty-thousand-dollar home. But my real life is here on the river. I been on the river ten years, and I like it real fine. It's a world of its own. It's a world I feel comfortable in. The Missouri is the friendliest river. Everybody knows everybody else. Nobody wants to cut your throat. I got a first cousin who's a captain on the Lower River. His mother was a real Christian woman. I mean, she had the power of prayer. When we were all growing up, my cousin he cut his middle finger off. The blood was gushing out, but his mother she started praying and the bleeding stopped. I mean it stopped. I remember seeing it with my own eyes. But most of those pilots on the Lower River, they don't like it much up here. This river is too fast for them. You know what they call the Missouri—they call it the Big Muddy. They used to say it was too thick to run and too thin to plow. But that ain't true no more. They've cleaned it up. But it's fast. I've averaged twelve to fourteen miles an hour going down with eight barges. That was high water—in May or June. Of course, I've also busted up some tows. It's three hundred and sixty-seven river miles from Kansas City to the mouth, just above St. Louis, and one trip I busted up seventeen times. It made a real long trip, chasing and catching and tying up those runaway barges. It took me seven days instead of two or three."

Evans sat up higher in his chair. He reached for a pair of binoculars and trained them down the river. There was a dark spot on the moving water far ahead. "Somebody coming," he said. "But we got the right-of-way. The down boat always has the right-of-way." He picked up a telephone and turned a radio dial. "*Lesta K.* to westbound tow coming into Wakenda Chute. Over."

A voice came out of a speaker: "*Belzoni* to *Lesta K.* How you doing, Dave?"

"Real fine, old buddy. How's it look down there?"

"Had a little trouble in Bushwacker. It's shallow, Dave. Real shallow."

"O.K., old buddy. I gotcha."

"Yeah. But, you know—no problem. How you want to pass?"

"I'll give you the bank. Port to port. One whistle."

"Gotcha, Dave. Say hello to everybody."

"Real fine, Skip. Will do. And the same to you."

I watched the *Belzoni* coming. It loomed slowly into shape. It came creeping up along the shore on the left behind a tow of eight barges. One of them carried a massive angularity of structural steel—a section of a bridge. Evans pulled a single blast on the whistle. The *Belzoni* replied. We came closely abreast, the *Lesta K.* moving at what looked like breakneck speed. Evans jumped out of his chair and stepped out on the bridge and waved. A man in a white shirt with the tails hanging loose waved back from the bridge of the *Belzoni*.

The river stretched bright and empty again. The green shores—bluff and bottom, bottom and bluff—ran on and on and on. I watched a flight of seven sandhill cranes flapping from shoal to shoal. There was a volume of charts on the bench where I sat: *Missouri River Navigation Charts: Kansas City, Missouri, to the Mouth*. Every bend, every crossing, every light was marked. I turned the pages, following the names downriver. Like all place names, they were a kind of poetry. Teteseau, Chamois, Cote Sans Dessein, Creve Coeur, St. Aubert, Auxvasse, Gasconade, Bonhomme. Tamerlane, Amazon, Malta, Euphrase, Miami, Berger, Bernheimer, Hermann, Berlin. Slaughterhouse, Plow Boy, Bushwacker, Rising Creek, Cowmire, Centaur, Pelican. The afternoon crawled peacefully away. Wilhoite, Lupus, Mullanphy, Diana.

I saw just three towns between Kansas City and the river mouth, below St. Charles. I had a passing view of the once premier port of Boonville (where in October of 1864 Price's Confederate Missourians, marching victoriously up the river to Gettysburgian defeat in the three-day Battle of Westport, paused for a spell of roistering rest, one of them leaving behind an unfinished letter: "Wee hav plenty of corn bred and pore beefe to eat and sasafras tee to drink"); Jefferson City, the capital (with the lanterned dome of the state capitol, the mansard roof of the governor's mansion, and the battlements of the state penitentiary strung along a landscaped bluff); and the tidy red brick waterfront of the old German town of Hermann. We stopped at none of them, but a mile or two above Hermann the *Irene E.*, from Staude's Boat Supply Dock, came out to meet us. That was late Sunday afternoon. I stood with Malone at the galley door and watched the *Irene E.* approach. "Pete Staude is my grocery store," Malone said. "I give him an order on one trip and pick it up on the next. He's bringing me out just a few things now, but I got a big order for him. All the boats trade with Pete. He handles everything but liquor. He even does our laundry. And he's where we get our mail." The *Lesta K.* slowed to the speed of the current, and the *Irene E.* came alongside. Two after-watch deckhands made it secure. We floated on together. A man in a business suit handed up a heavy crate and a bundle of mail tied with string.

"I hope for once you brought me the right kind of peas," Malone said. "I mean them little ones, Pete."

"You got them, old buddy," Staude said. "And everything else you ordered."

"It better not be them big-as-chinaberry kind."

"I even got the Sunday paper for you," Staude said. "Now, who needs what?"

Somebody broke the string on the parcel and spread out the mail on the dining table. The crew, both watches —everybody but Evans, up in the pilothouse—crowded around. There were typewritten bills and business letters and letters addressed in pencil and big, thick letters in scented envelopes addressed in colored ink. The deckhand called Tear Drops had one of the scented letters, and he turned his back and stood in a corner to read it. Johnny Avent had three.

Before going down to bed that night, I went out on the

bridge for a breath of river air and heard a kind of music. It was a whining and whanging and thumping, and it came from the main deck, below. I leaned over the rail and looked down on Johnny Avent and two deckhands. Johnny was sitting on a box with the blade of a carpenter's saw bent against the deck like a musical saw, and he was tapping it with a hammer. The deckhands were dancing—stomping and whirling and clapping their hands. It gave me a curious feeling, a curious start of memory. I remembered a painting by the mid-nineteenth-century genre painter George Caleb Bingham called *The Jolly Flatboatmen*, which shows the long-haired crew of a river scow cavorting on deck to the music of a fiddler. I looked down at the whining saw and the capering deckhands, and wondered again at how little the river seemed to change.

After breakfast (pineapple juice, oatmeal, ham and eggs, and grits), I walked out to the head of the tow to watch the sun come up. The sky overhead was black and clear and full of stars, but a layer of fog hung, boiling like steam, on the river. I sat and watched the stars fade and the sky go gray and the first spread of pink appear. It was still dark, it still had the feel of night, and then suddenly it was morning. The sun was up, and the fog was thinning and opening and drifting away, and the grass along the steep right bank was dappled with dewy cobwebs.

I heard somebody coming up the middle of the tow. It was Johnny Avent, hunched under a braided ball of two-inch rope the size of a bushel basket. Behind him came the deckhand Polka Dots with another. They hung one ball over the side of the starboard barge and the other off the port barge. Johnny came over and sat down on the deck beside me. "Them?" he said. "They're bumpers. We hang them out whenever we go through a lock. On the Upper River and up on the Illinois, they're hanging there all the time. The Upper Mississippi is nothing but locks. There's only one lock on this run—the Chain of Rocks lock, just above St. Louis." He gave his cutthroat mustache a pull. "I guess you've heard of William Faulkner," he said. "And Eudora Welty? And William Alexander Percy? And Shelby Foote? And Hodding Carter? Then you probably know they're all Mississippians—and so am I. I come from Greenville. My daddy is port engineer for Port City. I guess that's why I'm on the river. He used to be a chief engineer, and all I ever heard since I was a little bitty boy was the river. I didn't always act like it, though. I studied architectural engineering at college—at Southern Mississippi—and I had a rock band there. I play piano and organ, and like that. I gigged in high school and college both. We played those long weekends. We'd play some college down in Louisiana and then cut over to Texas and come back by way of Alabama or Tennessee. I got me an ulcer, and my grades went down, so I finally quit. The other fellas, they're still playing, but my real world was always the river. I worked here summers, and I've been on the river full time since I got out of school last year. Captain Easy—that's what we call Captain Bills;

there's another captain we call Captain Rough—he's teaching me to be a pilot. I like the river, I like this peaceful life. It's peaceful, but it isn't lonely. I like the way you've always got somebody to horse around with and throw the bull with. And I like the money, too. I get twenty-seven eighty-five a day—that's the rate for a second mate—and it's all clear money, I mean, I haven't got anybody, and when I'm home I live with my daddy and mummy. I don't even smoke. It's nice to have that big old roll of money. You go in a local bar and start flashing a few fifties around, and those chicks, they kind of go for that. It's like being in the band again, the way those chicks come running, only better. You don't have to pack right up and drive to, like Shreveport. I like money. But, thank God, I didn't sell my body that time. The medical school down at Louisiana State was offering three hundred dollars apiece for bodies to be claimed after death, and five of us drove down to New Orleans. We wanted that easy money for partying. But then we found out they were going to tattoo something on your heel for identification. I didn't like the idea of some girl getting into bed and looking down and reading my heel and thinking I'd been stole from some morgue."

I dropped the sports section of yesterday's St. Louis *Post-Dispatch* back on the pilothouse bench. I got up and stood at the window. "It looks like the river is getting a little wider," I said.

"Wider?" Bills said.

"I don't know," I said. 'It just seems wider than it was."

"Yeah," he said. "Well, it *is* wider. It's just about twice as wide. But it's a different river. We come out of the Missouri at that big long bend back there. That was the mouth. This here is the Mississippi."

I left the *Lesta K.* on Monday afternoon at St. Louis. As we came out of the lock at Chain of Rocks, Bills received a radioed order to exchange his barges there for another tow and return with it upriver to Kansas City. The Port City Barge Line had made arrangements for me to continue my trip on another boat—the *National Progress*, of the National Marine Service, Inc., of St. Louis, H. P. Duplantis, captain. The *National Progress* was tied up just below the St. Louis waterfront, and the *Lesta K.* churned down there on its way to pick up its new tow—past the Eads Bridge (the first steel bridge built across the Mississippi, completed in 1874, built with arches high enough between the piers to clear the tall twin stacks of the paddlewheel steamers), past the new soaring Saarinen wishbone arch, past the anchored replica of the *Santa Maria*, past the five-deck excursion boat *Admiral*, past the floating restaurant *Huck Finn*, past the showboat *Goldenrod*. The *National Progress* stood offshore, behind a tow of four shining double-tank refrigerated anhydrous ammonia barges, flying the company's flag—a red beaver on a white background. We came alongside, and I stepped across the gap. A deckhand in bib overalls—a big, grumbling fat man—took me to my cabin and then on to the pilothouse. He climbed the steep stairs breathing hard and pulling at the seat of his pants. "I don't know about work clothes anymore," he said. "You can't get anything that will wear for more than forty-five minutes. I think the Mafia must have taken over the whole shebang."

The pilothouse was as loud and crowded as a cocktail party. There was Duplantis, a young Cajun with long black hair and bright blue eyes, sitting on the bench. There was the pilot, a young Mississippian named William McBunch, at the console. There was a refrigeration technician (anhydrous ammonia is ammonia liquefied by sub-zero cooling for safekeeping), a young Arkansan named Dennis Blackford. There was a deckhand from Texas making coffee at a little stove in a corner, and a deckhand from Missouri. The fat deckhand and I brought the number in the little room to seven. Everybody was smoking and drinking coffee and talking at the top of his voice.

". . . and married a fella from Texas."

"It's a funny thing—you meet a fella from Texas, and if you call him Tex, he kind of preens. But you meet a fella from Arkansas and you call him Arkie—well, you got a fight on your hands."

"You ask me, I'd rather have a sister in a whorehouse than a brother in Texas."

"I don't know why they call a Cajun a 'coon-ass.' I never ate coon in my life."

"The way I heard it, every time you mention Missouri, a jackass will kneel down and pray."

I sat down on the bench, and one of the deckhands brought me a cup of coffee. It was black and strong, and sharp with chicory. The deckhand leaned on the arm of the bench.

"That's coon-ass coffee," he said. "That's what they call it. And we make it drip. But every captain on this line has his own idea about how to make his coffee. One captain has me make it one spoon of Luzianne and then one spoon of Community, then another spoon of Luzianne and another one of Community. And so on. And it has to be just right or he gets as mad as a mule."

"I remember one time," Duplantis said. "We took a new cook on at Memphis. One of the deckhands came running up here to the pilothouse and he said, 'Oh, Jesus, Duke, you won't believe it but that new cook she's a girl.' Well, I'd heard of women cooks on the river—a few old widows. But he was right. She came up to report, and she was a young girl. Good-looking, too, and built real nice. She said she had an aunt who had cooked on towboats. She said she had taken home economics in high school, and her aunt had taught her the rest. The aunt had told her about the different watches and when they ate and the kind of food, and about accommodating the crew. I said, 'The what?' The men, she said—about going to bed with the men. However, she said, her aunt had told her not to play favorites. That could only cause trouble. She would take the fellas in turn when they wanted her. But she had one rule. Nobody but me was to know her last name or where she lived on shore. And that's the way it was. She accommodated the fellas—practically the whole boat. But then the trouble began. It was just what she had tried to avoid. Dissension. They all of them fell in love with her, or thought they had, and in no time at all everybody—even the married men—was unhappy and jealous and snarling at everybody else. So when we got up to Marseilles, Illinois, I had to put her ashore. She was a real nice girl—real likable, and a good cook, too. But she was strange—real strange. I remember her name. It was Shirley."

"It was Shirley Ann," the Missouri deckhand said.

I had supper that night with the after watch (fried country ham and redeye gravy, sweet potatoes, succotash, okra, banana cream pie) and then sat for a while on the texas deck and watched a new moon rise. I saw what the early-Victorian novelist Captain Frederick Marryat had seen before me—had seen almost a century and a half before: "I did not expect that the muddy Mississippi would be able to reflect the silver light of the moon; yet it did, and the effect was very beautiful. Truly it may be said of this river, as it is of many ladies, that it is a candle-light beauty." I went down to bed before nine. The nights are short when you are called for breakfast at five o'clock. My cabin was over the engine room, and I awoke a dozen times to the grinding roar of the engines backing and braking, but only for a moment. The usual engine sound —the steady forward thrust—was a soporific hum.

Duplantis was alone in the pilothouse but was talking on the telephone when I climbed the stairs after breakfast. I stopped at the door that opened onto the bridge.

The river was unmistakably the Mississippi now. It stretched a mile wide and infinitely on ahead. In the thin white early morning light, it might have been a lake. But the banks were still riverbanks—sandbars and willow flats, willow slopes and high cottonwood bluffs.

"Yeah," Duplantis said on the telephone. "I gotcha, man. I'll just keep paddling." He hung up, and turned. "There's fresh coffee there on the stove. Or if you'd rather have a Coke, there's some in the refrigerator underneath. And you can pour me some more coffee while you're at it." He was wearing dark glasses, and his long dark hair hung down across one eye. "That's Pond Lily Light over there on the Missouri side. We made good time last night, in spite of a lot of fog—better than sixty miles a watch. We're past Cape Girardeau and we're getting close to Cairo. It's interesting there, the way the Ohio comes in. A lot of pilots think the books have got the rivers wrong. You can see it here on this chart. The Mississippi comes in from the west and the Ohio comes down from the north, and after they meet you can see how the Mississippi bends and runs due south. A lot of the pilots think the Ohio is the main river and the Mississippi is the feeder— the tributary. I think they've got a point. And here comes the fella I was talking to."

The tow came distantly into view, hugging the high Missouri shore—a tiny white pilothouse rising behind an acreage of barges. It came close enough for me to make out the head of the tow: it spread five barges wide. I took up a pair of binoculars and read the name on the pilothouse: *Theresa Seley*. Duplantis pulled the whistle twice, for a starboard-to-starboard passing. The *Theresa Seley* replied in confirmation, and came slowly up and slowly abreast and past. Duplantis raised a hand in the ritual greeting. I counted the barges. The tow was five barges wide and six barges long—a total of thirty barges. It *was* an acreage. It was five acres of barges. And, at fifteen hundred tons per barge, it carried thirty-five thousand tons of cargo. It was more cargo than could be moved by rail on a freight train of three hundred cars.

"Fellas new on the river are scared of certain cargoes," Duplantis said. "It scares them to handle oil or petrochemicals—chemicals of any kind. Those things are dangerous. Anhydrous ammonia is dangerous. So you have to be careful. You have to follow the safety rules. But the kind of load that scares me most is something else entirely. If you noticed that boat, the *Theresa Seley*, he had a couple of deck barges loaded with river sand. That wet river sand is real unstable. It shifts. Even a gentle turn can shift the load, and a shift of fifteen hundred tons of sand—all that weight, with the buoyance all underneath—it can turn you right smack over. I've never had any trouble. I've never even come close, except once when I tried to keep from running down two measly little ducks. I've never had anything like a fire or explosion, but I had a tow one time where it would have been kind of interesting. That was up on the Upper River. I picked up a tow at St. Paul of eight barges of popping corn and a jumbo barge of soybean oil. All the way down to St. Louis, at every lock and every bend, I kept thinking, What if something happened? What if something exploded? What if we got hit by lightning? My God, the whole Middle West would be knee-deep in buttered popcorn!"

I left the *National Progress* around ten o'clock that morning off the village of Hickman, Kentucky, just north of the Tennessee line. The circumstances were much the same as those that had moved me to the *Progress* from the *Lesta K.*: an order had been telephoned to Duplantis to meet another National Marine Service towboat there—the *National Gateway*, Victor Wood, captain—transfer his tow to her, and return upriver to Hannibal. Arrangements had been made for me and the refrigeration technician, Blackford, to continue aboard the *Gateway*, destination Baton Rouge. The *Gateway*, built in 1966, was bigger and finer than the *Progress*, and my cabin was a guest stateroom—twin beds, a deep leather armchair, a reading lamp, a tiled bathroom hung with big thick towels. Across the passageway was a lounge for the crew, with a sofa, comfortable chairs, a television set, and a table piled with paperback books (including *Ada*, by Vladimir Nabokov, and Saul Bellow's *Herzog*) and copies of the Memphis *Press-Scimitar* and Hodding Carter's Greenville *Delta Democrat-Times*. The boat gave a shudder. I looked out the window. We were under way—behind a seven-barge tow of anhydrous ammonia and caustic soda, with red metal danger flags standing stiff on every barge. I found the stairs to the pilothouse and went up. Wood—thirty-eight, green-eyed, tousle-haired, unshaven, sockless—was at the console. A gray-haired deckhand with a sunken jaw was sitting on the bench.

". . . seniority," the deckhand said. "That's what they say. Thirty minutes of kissing ass will do you more good than thirty years of seniority."

"Yeah?" Wood said. "Well, I tell you what. How about you going over there to the stove and pouring everybody a nice little cup of coffee?"

We moved around an overgrown towhead island and into a long starboard crossing. The Missouri shore loomed and lifted, and through the trees I could see the slope of a field of stubble corn. A congregation of crows was busy among the rows. "My hometown isn't far from here," Woods said. "It wouldn't be more than thirty miles for one of those crows. Sikeston, Missouri—my daddy was a cotton farmer there. I never meant to go on the river. I guess I'd have to call it just an accident. But once I got started, I was hooked. It's another kind of life. It's like one of those drugs. There ain't no future and there ain't no past. There's nothing but the river. That's the way you get to feel. But the river has been good to me. There's enough here to keep you going. You start in decking, and if you've got enough smarts you try to climb. I'd come up to the pilothouse in my off-duty hours and watch the captain. That old man made a pilot out of me. He went back to the old river days when you could chew a man out, when you could make him feel like nothing—when you could kick him all over the deck. But he wasn't that kind of man. I learned everything from him. Any man is welcome in my pilothouse. He can come up and set and talk and enjoy the scenery any time his work is done or his watch is over. But I expect him not to abuse it. He's got to behave himself. There was a time when the river was my only home. I worked nine straight months on a boat without putting foot on shore. Me and another pilot bought a towboat and went into business on our own. I didn't have no children then, and my wife traveled with me most of the time. She really rowed the boat. She could have passed my pilot's license easier than I did. I kept at it for eight years, but it was hard work, running the boat and running the business, too. So one day I sold my share to my partner and went back to working for somebody else. But I come out ahead—I come out with my house paid for, and a nice little farm down in southern Missouri, and a couple of dollars in my pocket. The best thing about it was my wife got to understand the river. So she and I, we kind of understand each other. We don't have the trouble some fellas have. I wake up when I'm home at about three in the morning—I can't sleep no more. And my wife gets up and puts on that little housecoat and makes up a cup of coffee. The only thing she grumbles about is when I've got to have that little nap in the afternoon."

"My old lady won't let me sleep," the deckhand said. "When I'm at home, we don't do nothing but go."

"Yeah?" Wood said. "I don't even go to church no more. That preacher we got, he's always stopping me and telling me I have to come to church. I told him no sir. People think you're isolated here on the river. They mean isolated from the world, and that's true. But you're not isolated from yourself. You get close to yourself, you get to know your thoughts. I told the preacher, 'If you believe in a Supreme Being—and I do—you're closer to Him out here than in any old Baptist church.' The preacher don't bother me. I know what my own mind tells me. I don't have to have somebody tell me if I'm doing wrong. I'm a grown man. I know right and I know wrong, and I know it all by myself."

The cook on the *National Gateway* was a thin, stern, bald-headed man from Texas named W. B. Wimberly. He was a country cook, and the galley was a big room with the feel of a country kitchen. There was always a view through a double door that gave on the low main deck—a framed and changeless view of a slowly passing countryside: the lift of a grass-grown levee, a skiff pulled up on a mudbank, willow thicket and cottonwood grove, cattle grazing in a field. There was a big refrigerator, never locked, with iced tea and milk, with grapefruit juice and orange juice and tomato juice, with cold meat and cottage cheese and a bowl of hard-boiled eggs. There was a big table set for eight in the middle of the room with a crowded tray of condiments. All the usual things were there (ketchup, mustard, French dressing, chili sauce, peanut butter, steak sauce, jelly, honey), but there were also other delicacies—Frank's Red Hot Sauce, Bruce's Banana Peppers, Evangeline Gumbo Filé. I went down

to dinner that day with the chief engineer, the technician Blackford, three deckhands, and the pilot, a gray, quiet Louisianan of fifty named Pierre Bourgeois. We helped ourselves from the stove and a buffet counter. Nobody talked and everybody ate. I watched one of the deckhands eat a bowl of chicken fricassee, an inch-thick slab of pot roast, mashed potatoes and gravy, lima beans (spiced with Frank's Red Hot Sauce), carrots, spinach, two wedges of corn bread, combination salad, and a dish of butterscotch pudding. There was a bowl of hard-boiled eggs on the table. He ate one egg with his chicken fricassee and two more with his pot roast, and he washed it all down with two glasses of cherry Kool-Aid. Wimberly sat in a corner and smoked and turned the pages of the *National Insider* ("How Jackie Lives When Nobody Is Looking") and sternly watched us eat.

We finished and made way for the forward watch. The engineer went back to the engine room, Blackford went out on the tow to check the refrigeration, the deckhands went off to sand and paint the texas deck. Bourgeois went up to the pilothouse, and a few minutes later I joined him there. He reached under the console and handed me a big floppy copy of *Flood Control and Navigation Maps of the Mississippi River: Cairo, Illinois, to the Gulf of Mexico.* "This river is famous for its crazy bends," he said, "and the one we're coming to is just about the craziest. See where it's marked Kentucky Point on the chart—where the river goes into a horseshoe bend that takes a big nipple out of the Missouri side. That's the bend we're coming into now. That's the famous New Madrid Bend. This is where they had that earthquake back in the Daniel Boone days —back there in 1811 and 1812. They tell me the New Madrid earthquake was the worst we ever had in this country. The river turned red and twisted around and ran upstream. It made the famous Reelfoot Lake, over there in Tennessee, and it made this New Madrid Bend. It's a real mixup. Our left bank right now is Tennessee and the right bank is Missouri, but up ahead about a mile the left bank is Kentucky again. It's nineteen miles from where we are, just coming into the bend, to where we come out, but if I was to drop you off at the neck up there you could walk across to the other end in probably fifteen minutes. It ain't much more than a mile. Some people say why don't they make a cutoff, dig a canal across the neck, save a lot of time? I say they better not. They better not fool around with any of these bends. The bends make the pressure that keeps the water level up. If you dug a straight channel from here on down to the Gulf, you wouldn't have nothing but a ditch. The water would run right off, like water off a rock. The only thing I've got against these bends is that's where you meet the traffic. I know of two tows right now that are coming up this bend. It's like they *like* to bunch up."

Bourgeois reached for the telephone, and I reopened *Flood Control and Navigation Maps of the Mississippi River*. I looked again at Kentucky Point and its trans-planted piece of Kentucky, and then leafed on through the book. Kentucky Point was only one among many such geographical confusions. The turnings and re-turnings of the Lower River have undone boundary lines all the way down to the Gulf. Part of Tipton County, Tennessee, now finds itself on the Arkansas side of the river, and part of Mississippi County, Arkansas, is on the Tennessee side. Part of Tunica County, Mississippi, is embedded in Lee County, Arkansas, and a good part of Lee County is over in Tunica County. Part of East Carroll Parish, Louisiana, has shifted across to Mississippi, and there is much of Mississippi isolated here and there along the Louisiana shore. I thought of Mark Twain's account of this phenom-enon in *Life on the Mississippi*. "The town of Delta," he reported, "used to be three miles below Vicksburg: a re-cent cut-off has radically changed the position, and Delta is now *two miles above* Vicksburg." I found Delta (Louisiana) on my map. It is now—almost a hundred years later—neither above nor below Vicksburg. It is directly across the river from that city, and two full miles to the west.

It was long after dark when we came into the harbor at Memphis. We took on supplies and mail from another floating ship chandlery, and Bourgeois went ashore to fly home for his fifteen days of leave. He was replaced by another Louisianan, a man named William Reeves. But I slept through all this and first heard about it from Wood the next morning, after breakfast. "Only that ain't what we call it," he said. "We don't call Memphis by its name. We call it Big Shelby. Shelby is the name of the county it's in. I don't know what the reason is. It probably goes way back to the very early days. There's a lot of traditions like that on the river. There's a crossing down near Battle Axe Bend that the chart calls Bordeaux Crossing. But what we call it on the river is Boodrow Crossing. And coming into Baton Rouge there's a point named Free Nigger Point. That's always been the name, and it don't mean nothing at all. It's just a name. But last year they changed it on the map to Free Negro Point. That made me kind of laugh. It made me think of our church back home. It was built back in my granddaddy's time. He was the town doctor and also the Baptist preacher, and he got the church built cheap out of slabs from that little sawmill they had. So everybody called it Slab Shanty Church. Then back when I was growing up—back in the nineteen-forties—the congregation raised some money and built a nice big new brick church. They named it the Union Grove Baptist Church. But you know what everybody calls it? Even the preacher? They call it Slab Shanty Church."

I went out on the tow that afternoon with Blackford. Unescorted idlers are not permitted on red-flag barges, and I went with his permission and equipped (as regulations require) with a life jacket. We walked along the echoing metal decks between the high-humped anhydrous ammonia tanks. "It's easy enough to explain," he said. "All you got to do is maintain the temperature in the tanks at minus twenty-eight degrees. That keeps the ammonia liquid and under control. When the temperature rises, it begins to vaporize. We run the vapor through the refrigeration unit and it liquefies again. I like this kind of work, and I like it on the river. I like those fifteen days on shore, too. I don't have a family. But I like to get cleaned up and move into a motel and go partying around St. Louis. But by the time my leave is over, I'm just about ready to come back. I'm like homesick for the river." Blackford left me at the head of the tow. He turned back to check his refrigeration units, and I sat down in the sun below a drooping company beaver flag and watched the river spreading and bending on ahead. And the traffic. There was a tow approaching now at almost every bend. We passed the *Sebring* (on two whistles) with four oil and chemical barges. We passed the *Ole Miss* (two whistles) with twenty hopper barges. We passed the *Franklin Pierce* (one whistle) with four petroleum barges and five jumbo hoppers. The sunlight began to dim. There were clouds building up to the west and south. Blackford came up and sat down and smoked a cigarette and carefully ground it out, and then we walked back to the boat. The clouds had gathered overhead, and the river looked dark and heavy. The banks looked far away.

We were eating supper when the rain began. It was almost dark, and the air was very still. It was a thin, drifting, drizzly rain, and it hung in the air like mist. "That was the forecast," Wood said. "There's some kind of a depression down in the Gulf. But there aren't many pilots that enjoy a rainy night on the river. Rain makes everything hard. If it's bad, it knocks the radar out, and if there's a lot of wind, it's worse. It kicks up a chop so you can't hardly see the buoys. It's almost as bad as fog."

"You ever been up there on the Ohio, Cap?" one of the deckhands said. "Where they got that Haunted Hollow Point? They say you're coming along on a bad night and you'll see the running lights of a boat. But you get just so close and they disappear on you."

"Yeah?" Wood said. "Well, if that ever happened to me, I'd give him a whistle and plenty of room. I wouldn't take no chances on him being a ghost."

The rain dripped down all night, and it was drizzling at breakfast on Thursday morning. But we were still moving. We were due in Baton Rouge sometime that night, and we were more or less on schedule. Then, around eleven o'clock, the drizzle stiffened into rain, and the wind began to blow. The rain drummed down on the open decks and blew in at the windows in sheets. I was watching it from the bench in the pilothouse just after dinner when a message came over the radio from the company office in St. Louis: "Attention, *National Gateway*. There is a storm moving into Louisiana from the Gulf. We do not want you to go past Natchez. Do not go past Natchez until further notice. Repeat. Stop at Natchez."

The relief captain, Reeves, was at the console. He was a big man in his middle fifties, with a big belly and a big, rough, smiling face. He acknowledged the order in a slow, untroubled voice. He hung up and reached for a cigarette. "You hear that?" he said. "Well, I was just thinking the

same myself. I didn't think this was any ordinary squall. I thought it looked kind of bad. But I know a good place to tie up at Natchez. That is, if somebody else ain't already beat me to it. And if I don't stub my toe getting there. I don't know. Look at that son of a bitch out there—that's what I call choppy water. We passed a tow just before you come up here that said they'd had some trouble down around Rifle Point, and that's exactly where we're coming to right now. I don't know if we're even going to make it. Just look at that rain. I can't hardly see a goddam thing. Look at them buoys, the way they're jumping around. You can't tell red from black. Well, I know one thing—I'm sure as hell not going down through Natchez. I sure don't want to run that bridge down there today. The place I got in mind is at the upper end of town. It's on the Louisiana side. But what if somebody's got it? I sure don't see no traffic. And there's a fella tied up over there. It looks like everybody is already tied up but us."

Reeves put out his cigarette. He picked up the binoculars and gazed out through the streaming glass. He put the binoculars down and lighted another cigarette. "Well, it won't be long now," he said. "That's Magnolia Bluff beginning over there. That's where those kids found all that money that time. They were playing along the shore and they saw something laying in the water and they fished it out and it was a coffee can full of silver dimes. Son of a bitch—you know what I think? I think I'd better start looking right now for a tree to tie up to. I got a feeling my place is took. I don't see a tree that will hold me. I don't see no trees at all. I don't see nothing but willow sprouts. And I sure wouldn't lay up like that fella over there at that towhead. He'll have some trouble getting off. But it ain't as bad as it was. See how that bluff has cut off the wind. But I don't know. There just ain't no real trees. And—son of a bitch. What did I tell you? There's my place and there's a fella in it. You know something? I'm going to have to try and run that goddam bridge."

I stood up for a better view. An old brick building appeared low down on the Mississippi shore. A street climbed up the bluff behind it. There were rooftops showing along the top of the bluff. That was Natchez. We came around a bend. A bridge loomed up through the rain. The channel marker led between two middle piers. The gap didn't look much wider than our tow. But Reeves didn't head for the channel. He pulled the head of the tow far off to the left, angling toward the Natchez shore, running straight at a string of barges moored along the face of a wharf. The bridge widened and rose higher overhead. An orange trailer truck was moving slowly across the bridge in the driving, blinding rain. Then the string of moored barges began to swing away—swing off to the left, and suddenly out of sight behind the big stone face of a pier— and we were back in the channel and sliding under the bridge and plunging out on the other side.

"Son of a bitch," Reeves said. He reached for another cigarette. "We made it. We got through there real fine. But I have to thank that Natchez bluff. I'd never made it

with that wind hitting me. But goddam it—I still got to find me a place to park. I can't keep rolling along half-blind like this. But I don't know. Everywhere I see a likely looking tree there's a fella already tied up to it. No, sir. I ain't never had this kind of trouble trying to find a place to tie up. There's nothing on this left bank—nothing open, anyway. I wonder should I go over there to the right bank and take a look? I sure can't see from here. Maybe if I got real close—but I can't. It's too shallow. See that black buoy. It's all of it shoal over there. There's nothing to do but keep going. I never saw anything like this in my whole damn life. Every tree got a barge tied to it. And where there ain't any barges there's nothing but levee bank. I don't know where we're going. I don't know what we're going to do. And we got a fifty-mile wind coming at us. Look at them trees, how they're bending. I swear to God, I just don't know. They told me stop at Natchez, and here we are still going. Goddam—there's Destruction Landing over yonder, and that's St. Catherine Bend just ahead. We're way below Natchez. We're fifteen miles below. I got to do something soon. I think I'll try right now. I sure would hate to have this tow bust up. What I'm going to do is go into that right bank there. I don't think much of the trees, but it's deep enough, and it even looks like it might be a little bit slack. I do believe I've found me a place. I do believe I have." He picked up the intercom microphone. "Angelo? Frank? All right, fellas—let's go."

We moved into a right-hand crossing, back toward

Louisiana. The only visible buoy was a red buoy a hundred yards or so from shore. Beyond it was a kind of cove, a little indentation in a bank of crumbling mud, and above the bank was a grove of tall, feathery willows. The trees were thrashing, bending almost double. Three deckhands in hooded yellow slickers came humping out on the main deck down below. They ducked across the deck, heads down and slickers flapping, and up a ladder to the stern of the starboard ammonia barge, and on to a coil of heavy mooring line. The sound of the engines changed to the vibrating roar of reverse. Reeves was standing now, leaning across the console, peering. We slid—every deck and bulkhead clanging against the wind and the current—half-broadside into the bank. The deckhands ran out a wooden gangplank. They went down the plank, hauling the line, and into the mud and up the bank to the trees. The trees leaned flat in a wilder gust, and two of them splintered and broke. The feathery top of one lifted high in the air. It sailed away like a gull. The deckhands struggled back aboard and broke out another line. The engines turned gently over in a slow, braking reverse. The rain came down and the mudbank melted and crumbled and the willows thrashed in the wind. But we were out of it now. We were out of the current, out of the pull of the river, sitting safe on a sheltered shore. Reeves turned away from the console. He walked back to the stove and picked up the coffeepot. "I'm going to have some coffee," he said. "How about you?"

The storm was almost over by the time I went down to bed that night. The rain had ended and the wind had dropped, and I could see the new moon racing through the last of the clouds and the deep blue sky opening up beyond. But the river still looked and sounded rough, and we were still moored along the mudbank. I lay in the dark and listened to the river and the sound of the engines still clanking away in reverse. A voice in the passageway said, "Five feet on the gauge at St. Louis." I dozed, and suddenly awoke. It was still dark—I had dozed for only a moment—but the engines had a different sound. I sat up and looked out the window. The mudbank was gone. We were well out on the river, and moving. I was in no hurry to get to Baton Rouge. But life on the river is movement, and it was good to be moving again. I rolled over and went back to sleep.

The Grower's Shadow

It is four o'clock on a warm spring afternoon, and I am sitting at the counter of the Mobil Cafe in the crossroads hamlet of Wilder, Idaho, in the Canyon County flats of the Snake River Valley, some thirty miles west of Boise. I am sitting with the chief Canyon County agent. He is a big, easy, weathered man of fifty-four named Merle R. Samson, and we have stopped here for a cup of coffee after a day in an air-conditioned pickup truck, poking around a dusty countryside of farms and orchards and distant mountains. The Cafe is full of farmers in bib overalls and pointed boots. Samson is known to many of them, and they nod and call him by name. Most of the farmers are white, but two are Japanese and one is a dark-skinned Mexican. They are drinking the watery café coffee and talking in voices that would carry across a feedlot.

". . . malathion."

"Yes, sir. I mean No. 1 Idaho bakers."

"No, by God. What it turned out to be was the *webworm*."

"That's right. Sixty cents a hundredweight to the grower."

"You want to know what I think of malathion? I'd sooner *pee* on my alfalfa."

"Well, two days later he was down at Salt Lake City, and he walked into the Safeway store, and son of a bitch —they were selling the same potatoes there at the equivalent of thirteen dollars a hundredweight."

"And now the bastards say I can't use dieldrin. I say we

ought to dump some dieldrin on the goddam ecologists."

"It's all those sons of bitches in between. They got their hand in *everybody's* pocket."

A county agent is the representative, at the barnyard level, of the Coöperative (state and federal) Agricultural Extension Service. It is he who brings to the farmer the fully ripened fruits of agronomical research. The county served by Samson and four other agents—an entomologist and three specialists in crops and cattle—plus two home economists is an exemplar of that service. Canyon is the leading agricultural county in Idaho, and, with an annual farm income of more than seventy-eight million dollars, derived from a cornucopia of crops—sugar beets, apples, sweet-corn seed, hops, potatoes, alfalfa seed, cattle, peppermint, red-clover seed, wheat, onions, lima-bean seed, cherries, milk, prunes, barley, alfalfa hay, spinach, peaches, popcorn—it is one of the most productive counties in the nation. That was why I was there.

The office of the Canyon County agent is in Caldwell (pop. 14,219), the Canyon County seat. It is situated on the lumberyard-and-warehouse side of the Union Pacific tracks, and occupies a nest of low-ceilinged rooms on the second floor of a two-story stucco building that was once a garage. The ground floor houses the A-Gem Supply Company. A long flight of steps at one end of the building leads steeply up to a labyrinthine corridor lined with open doors and racks of United States Department of Agriculture publications: *Controlling the Mexican Bean Beetle, Diseases of Mint, A Career for Me in Agriculture, Growing Carrot Seed in Idaho.* I had climbed those steps for the first time at around nine o'clock that morning. Samson's room was the first open door on the left. He was there, at his desk, talking on the telephone. He looked up and smiled and pointed to a chair. I removed a pile of papers and an apple—a big red, shiny Delicious apple—to the top of a filing cabinet and sat down. Through the window there was a view of a warehouse roof, and above the roof was an immensity of sky—the wide blue sky of the mountain West.

"And how about the leaves?" Samson was saying on the telephone. "Right. It looks a lot like wild parsley. Or wild carrot. And the root is very often mistaken for wild parsnip. . . . Well, that's what it sounds like to me. I think you've got yourself some poison hemlock there. . . . No, you sure don't. . . . You bet it is—it's very toxic. What I think you better do is fence that area off and treat it with a chemical weed killer, maybe 2,4-d. . . . Right. And the sooner the better."

Samson hung up and swung around in his chair. His face was lined and deeply tanned. "Well," he said, and lighted a cigarette. "I'll tell you the truth. That's the only thing I don't much like about this job. I mean the telephone. I'm a county agent that likes to be out in the country. But I guess it could be worse. I know it could. I quit the Service back in 1951 and tried it out in the world. I went into the feed-and-grain business. I stayed out there for three years, and that was enough. I was more than ready to come back. County agents don't often get rich, but they get a lot of real job satisfaction—they're giving instead of taking. And they don't have to sit at a desk all day. At least, not every day."

The telephone rang. Samson swung back to his desk. He answered and listened and brightened. "Right," he said. "You bet I do—I was down there a couple of days ago. But it depends on what you want. You've got a good location there. The conditions are very good. If you want to try a legume, I'll have to suggest alfalfa. You might try mixing alfalfa and orchard grass. . . . You bet. It makes a real fine permanent pasture. . . . Oh, I don't know—I guess forty-sixty would be about the best proportion. Or you could try just a sprinkling of alfalfa and the rest grass. Or all grass. . . . Right. And, of course, grass is a good soil builder. But if you're going to broadcast it, I'd increase that just a little—maybe ten pounds to the acre. . . . Well, sure. And with an all-grass pasture you don't have to worry about bloat in your cows. . . . You bet."

Samson hung up. He sat for a moment, rubbing his left ear. "I guess I've been pretty lucky," he said. "I know what I want, and I've got it. I was born and raised in Idaho, and, except for the Navy Air Corps in the Second World War, I've never had to leave it. I got my B.S. at the university, up at Moscow. I've worked up there, in Latah County, and I've worked in the east, around Poca-tello. I've been all over the state. And Canyon County here is the best of Idaho. They call this Treasure Valley. We've got a diversity of crops which I doubt can be matched anywhere. That makes it interesting. I like a little variety. But we've got some specialties, too. We're the No. 1 county in the country—in the whole United States—in sweet-corn-seed production. And in alfalfa seed. And red-clover seed. And mixed grains. We're No. 5 in sugar beets. We're way up in dairy production. And so on. We've never had a crop failure. There's been some reduced yields here, but never an out-and-out failure. And it all began from nothing. Sixty years ago, this county was a wasteland. It was nothing but sagebrush desert. We get only about eight inches of rain a year. It was irriga-tion that made the difference, of course. We have plenty of underground water here, but we don't irrigate with that. We don't mine our underground reserves, the way some states are doing. The water we use is mountain snow-melt, impounded in storage lakes."

The telephone rang. Samson turned and looked at it. But he answered it on the third ring. "Oh," he said. "How you doing? . . . Right. . . . Yes, so I understand. . . . That's right. . . . Well, you've sprayed enough acreage to know. . . . You bet." He laughed. "But just remember, Roy. Remember what Hugh Homan told you about mala-thion and the paint on automobiles. It acts like a solvent."

Samson hung up. "That's enough," he said. He stood up. "Let's get out of here. Let's go see how the season is going. I'll take you for a little drive."

Hugh Homan is the entomologist assigned to Canyon County. I met him the following morning—a thickset man of thirty-eight with a hard blue jaw and heavy black brows and sideburns. He invited me to join him on a round of professional calls. We drove out of town on a wide gravel road in a dirty white Volkswagen with a big can of Treflan weed killer bouncing around in back. The sky overhead was fresh and blue, but there were cloudy mountains on the horizon. Homan's right hand, on the wheel, was missing the thumb and forefinger. "This fellow I want to see first is a fruitgrower named Norman Vermeer," he said. "He's got a problem with sandburs in one of his orchards. I should have seen him yesterday, but I had to go over to Boise and testify in an accident case. A farmer was burning a crop residue, and the smoke blew across the road, and a driver came along and couldn't see, and stopped. Another car came up and didn't see him sitting there, and smashed into him. Killed him. So his family is suing the farmer for negligence. I testified on farming practices. Burning crop residue instead of tilling it back into the soil is bad farming. But I had to testify that they do it all the time. It's common practice. Farming is a hazardous occupation, and one big reason is carelessness. I grew up on a farm just north of here, in Payette County, and I learned my lesson early. I was just sixteen when I lost my fingers. I was running a balky old corn picker, and I tried to reach under the rollers to fix something without turning off the engine. The only lucky thing was, I happen to be left-handed."

We slowed to turn off onto a bumpy lane, and my window filled with a sudden sugary jasmine smell of wild currant. There was a fence-line thicket of blossoming bushes just across the road. A yellow-headed blackbird was perched on one of the flowering branches.

"Now, there's a pretty sight," Homan said.

"The blackbird?" I said.

"What?" he said. "Oh—heck no. I mean that old rooster pheasant marching across that field. I've got a date with him for next fall. This is real good country here. I mean for farming *and* living. We start off in September with a season on doves. Then sage grouse. Then quail: bobwhite and mountain and valley—all three. Then pheasant. Then, up in the hills, chukar and Hungarian partridge. That's good, hard hunting. Then ducks and geese down along the river. Then, later on, if you've got the ambition to pack into the mountains, there's elk. I reload my own shotgun shells, and last fall I used a hundred pounds of lead, in one-and-a-quarter-ounce shot. So you can see I did a little bit of shooting. But I don't have any trouble enjoying my weekends any time of the year. We've got trout fishing in the spring, and there's bass and perch in the lakes in summer. And there's good skiing up in the mountains. This isn't just the place where I was born and raised. This country here is my *home*."

We pulled into a rutted driveway between a big storage barn and a little white house in a somber grove of pines. Beyond the drive were the pink-canopied aisles of a peach orchard. A tall, blond smiling young man came out through the pines to meet us. He was Vermeer.

"Hugh," he said. "This sandbur situation here is serious.

Those little farmers are mean. They made trouble for me with my pickers last fall. You know those fishhook barbs—they'll dig right through your pants. My pickers couldn't stand it. And you know about good pickers."

"I know they're hard to get," Homan said. "But maybe I can help. Anyway, I brought you this can of Treflan. I want you to try it. One quart to the acre in forty gallons of water. Then we'll see. Where are they giving you trouble—in your peach orchard there?"

"They're in my plums. You want to take a look?"

"You bet. Your peaches look good, Norman. Did you light for that frost back there?"

"I probably should have. I took a chance. And for once I was lucky. I understand they're hurting bad on stone fruits up in Washington."

"So I hear."

Vermeer laughed. "Well, you know how we feel about that. We sit down every night and pray that Washington freezes out. Then we might have a chance to make some money."

"Hey," Homan said. "You really do have some sandburs here."

"They're healthy little farmers," Vermeer said. "And these plums are one of my best crops. They all go back to New York—they're all for the kosher market."

"That's a good contract market."

"It is—but, you know, I wonder about those people back there. They buy all the plums I can grow, but they've never tasted a real plum. I mean a ripe plum. To get them there in the condition the market wants, I've got to pick them three weeks early. But they're really good plums when they ripen on the tree. The pickers always leave a few on every tree for us."

"The consumer is the boss."

"That's the trouble. The consumer eats with her eyes. It's funny, isn't it? She won't buy an apple unless it looks like a picture. It has to be big and red and shiny. But you and I and every grower knows that a little green adds flavor, and the redder the skin the tougher it is. I doubt if I'd even grow a red Delicious if she didn't make me. I might grow Jonathans or Rome Beauties. This is the best Rome country in the world."

"She'll change her mind someday," Homan said. "The fashion will turn to something else. Remember the Baldwin and the McIntosh and the old Arkansas Black."

"I know she'll change," Vermeer said. "And then I'll have to pull out half of my orchard."

We followed a long flat, empty blacktop road. Flanking it were boundless potato fields. Then the land began to dip. We passed a hopyard, with its twenty-foot poles and overhead wires and clustering, climbing vines. We came around the slope of a crumbling, sunbaked butte. We passed a barn remodeled into a house, and then a leafy alfalfa field. We turned into a drive at a gray shingle house with a straggle of sheds and shacks in back. There was a sound of hammering from behind the sheds.

Homan shut off the engine and leaned on the wheel.

"This is a highly successful alfalfa-seed operation," he said. "It's a partnership. A couple named Trueblood live in that barn over there, and an old batch named Wally Burrill lives here. Bud Trueblood grows the alfalfa, and Wally raises the bees. Alfalfa is pollinated by a species of leaf-cutter bee. Those sheds with the open fronts are mobile bee boxes. Domesticated leaf-cutter bees don't live in hives. They nest in the holes of perforated boards called bee boards. The average board will have around two thousand holes, and there are usually twelve cells—twelve bees—to the hole. The bees are kept in refrigerated hibernation until just before blossomtime. Then the boards are hung in the sheds and hauled out to the field. Alfalfa pollination requires a lot of bees—between seven and ten thousand to the acre. And only the females work. This kind of beekeeping is full of problems. But that isn't why I'm here. There isn't much that I can teach Wally and Bud about their business. They're exceptional. What usually happens, I learn from them. So I like to stop by whenever I'm around this part of the county. And Mary Trueblood is a real good cook."

The hammering stopped, and a gray-haired man with a bony face and rimless glasses appeared. "I heard you drive in," he said, "but I was up on the roof of a shed. I've finally built me some sheds I like."

"I was looking at that new one over there," Homan said. "How come you're using planks?"

"Oh, Jesus," Burrill said. "I got sick of that goddam plywood. It's so goddam phony. But that isn't the only difference. These new sheds have all got double roofs for good ventilation. I want to make those little bastards comfortable. And I'm hinging the bottom planks on all three walls for the same reason. They're just as sensitive to heat as they are to cold."

"A lot of growers don't seem to realize that," Homan said. "They have to learn the hard way."

"You're goddam right," Burrill said. "A bee don't come alive until the temperature gets to seventy plus, and he'll die at one hundred and five. You've got to watch the little bastards. I remember one morning a couple of years ago I was making a round of my sheds. The early sun was shining in the open fronts, and the temperature up at board level—about chest level—was seventy-one degrees, and the bees were dropping out of their holes. But the floor in the sheds was still cold, and they lay there turning numb. What I did was grab a broom and race around sweeping them out—sweeping them out into the sun. And son of a bitch—it only took a minute of sunshine. They sat up and flew off to start making me some money. I could have lost every goddam bee I had."

"A lot of people have," Homan said.

Homan and I had noon dinner with the Truebloods and Wally Burrill in Mary Trueblood's kitchen. The Truebloods are in their fifties. She is a pretty woman with soft gray hair, and he is tall and lanky and burned to leather. We sat in comfortable chairs at a long table wtih a centerpiece of red tulips. We began with roast lamb, baked potatoes, and fresh green asparagus, and finished with cherry pie and coffee. The asparagus had been cut (by Mrs. Trueblood) only that morning from a volunteer stand along a fencerow. In Canyon County, asparagus is a weed. The seeds are spread by birds, and the plants thrive wherever they can escape cultivation—in the shelter of fences and around the trunks of orchard trees.

"I remember when we took out our orchard up home," Homan said. "My job was to dig up the asparagus roots around the trees. Those roots were harder to get out than the stumps."

"I've broken a plow on asparagus roots," Trueblood said. "I detest it with a purple passion. Except when it's here on my plate."

The stove on which the asparagus, and everything else, was cooked was a coal stove—a big black cast-iron turn-of-the-century Majestic range.

"I spent years finding that stove," Mrs. Trueblood said. "I wouldn't cook on anything else. Coal heat is the perfect cooking heat. Of course, it's more trouble than gas or electricity, but that's true of so *many* things. So many good things take trouble. Like this homemade bread we're eating. And homemade pie. And homegrown vegetables. I love my Majestic stove. And one day when I was up in Bud's mother's attic, I found another treasure. It's hanging there over the stove: *The Majestic Cook Book.*"

"Hell's bells," Burrill said. "Everything worthwhile takes trouble."

"I had to learn that for myself," Trueblood said. "I had to go all the way to college to find out how to farm.

My father sure never taught me. He farmed on the principle of let's hurry up and make as much as we can right now and never mind what happens to the soil. It never occurred to him to give nature half a chance. But the things I finally learned weren't new. A year or two ago, I picked up a copy of the Department of Agriculture *Yearbook* for 1902—and it's all in there. Crop rotation. Soil conservation. Cultivation. The Extension Service tried to teach it to my dad, but he couldn't be bothered. He couldn't even be bothered to irrigate right. It was easier to overwater, so he leached his soil away."

"There are still a lot of farmers like your dad," Homan said. "We've worked out a little table at the office. We figure that maybe two per cent of the farmers are truly receptive to new ideas. They're men like you and Wally. We call them innovators. Then comes a group of fifteen per cent that we call early adapters. Then comes a middle group of sixty per cent. They're the regular majority. They come in when the ideas are pretty well established. Another fifteen per cent are the late adapters. They're the ones that say, 'Hell, I'm doing all right, these new ideas are probably just a flash in the pan, so I guess I'll wait and see.' And then there's those that never adapt."

"We got one of those bastards for a neighbor," Burrill said. "He told me he wouldn't think of using fertilizer. He said it made the weeds grow too fast."

"A lot of farmers come to our meetings just to get away from their wives," Homan said. "Or maybe to see their friends. They don't even try to learn."

"Learning is hard work," Trueblood said. "But, good Lord, so is chukar hunting."

The Snake River swings up from the south a mile or two west of the Trueblood farm, and Homan and I crossed it there on the Homedale Bridge. The river was fast and muddy, with many brushy islands, and the banks were lined with drooping willows. On the other side of the river, beyond the one-street village of Homedale, the road began to rise. Our destination was a hilltop orchard owned by a man named Shults. "Garfield Shults," Homan said. "He called me out here a couple of weeks ago for advice on spraying his apple trees for scale. I want to see how good a job he did. Garfield sells all his fruit at retail. He's an old-fashioned door-to-door peddler, and he makes enough to live the way he wants to. His real interest is grafting—experimenting with different species and varieties. I met a man from Cornell at the annual meeting of the Entomological Society of America last year. 'So you're from Idaho,' he said. 'I wonder if you know a man named Garfield Shults. He just wrote and asked me for some New York McIntosh slips.' Garfield's known from coast to coast."

Shults's orchard was a jungle. Towering, tortured, unpruned apple trees. Bushy pears and peaches and plums. Reedlike saplings half buried in thigh-high grass. We found Shults down on his knees hacking at the roots of an apricot stump. He stood up to greet us—a small, ragged, beaming man in a khaki sun helmet. "Hugh," he said. "You know something? I think that spray did good."

"I think so, too," Homan said. "All the scale I've seen is dead." He rubbed his hand along an apple branch. "Nothing left but dust."

"And that tree there was just about lathered with them."

"That's right. But, my God, Garfield—when are you going to mow this grass? This is no way to grow fruit."

"Oh, I'm going to mow it. Don't worry about that. But right now I've got something to show you. Here's a row that's really dizzy. I've got prune plums growing on an apricot tree. The way I figure—if the prunes freeze out, I've still got a crop of apricots."

"Right."

"This whole section is dizzy. This dizzy-looking tree is my experimental laboratory. I've got it growing seven or eight different apples—Roanoke from Virginia, McIntosh from New York, Splendor from New Zealand, and Spies and Jonathans and Romes. And I've got a mystery apple here. I crossed a red and a golden Delicious. It's got those wide Delicious shoulders. But it's pink, Hugh—it's just as pink as a peach blossom. Oh, and here's a berserk Bartlett pear. Now, what the heck did I do here? I've forgotten, except that it keeps as good as a Bosc. And here's another berserk tree where I've forgotten exactly what I did. But I'll be watching it. I'll find out in a couple of months. That's half the fun. Is it going to be something delectable? Or merely edible? Or do you feed it to the horses? But I wanted to ask you, Hugh. What am I going to do about those bugs?"

"I keep telling you, Garfield. We can't get rid of bugs. We can't *eradicate* them. We don't even want to. They've got their place."

"O.K. But what do I *do?*"

"You learn to live with them, Garfield."

Homan and I climbed back up through the overgrown aisles in a susurration of bees. We came out of the orchard dusk and into the hilltop afternoon. "Garfield is like so many farmers," Homan said. "They're chemical activists. We're trying hard to change all that. We're trying to teach them that insecticides are the last resort. They mean you've failed at proper control—biological control. Our target orchard insect is the codling moth. It puts the worm in the apple. But when we first learned how to kill the codling moth chemically, we also killed the predators of the spider mite, and the spider mite became a very serious problem. Then we started using less toxic stuff on the codling moth and spared the predators. Now we're working to control the codling moth by confusing him at breeding time with a synthetic female scent. I think the farmers are beginning to listen to us. Not because they're fascinated by the idea of biological control. They listen because they're businessmen, and insecticides cost money. They cost a lot of money."

The senior home economist in the Canyon County office is a tall, fair, blue-eyed woman of thirty named Beverly Montgomery. Mrs. Montgomery and I had a cup of coffee together in her office. It is a windowless room with a desk, a filing cabinet, and a big 4-H poster: "I pledge my Head to clearer thinking, my Heart to greater loyalty, my Hands to larger service, and my Health to better living, for my Club, my Community, and my Country." "My work is mostly with our nutrition-education program," she said. "This is a rich county in many ways, but we have a lot of low-income families—welfare and food-stamp people. We have poor white people and poor Mexicans. Our Japanese families all seem to be self-sufficient. I would say that at least one-third of our population needs nutritional guidance. It's distressing how poorly informed they are, and how improvident. At the first of the month, when they have some money, they eat well. I mean, by their standards—hamburgers, hot dogs, potato chips, Cokes, and the snack foods they see advertised on television. Television is a problem. It's the only source of information that these people have. They don't read newspapers or magazines, and few of them have had much schooling. Television commercials are their guides to living. Well, they tend to blow their budget in the first two weeks of the month. The third week is pretty tight. And by the fourth week they are often quite literally down to plain rice or macaroni. With no sauce, no butter—nothing. Then they get their checks or stamps, and they're so hungry for good food they'll blow it again on impulse—on strawberries at seventy-nine cents a pound, or half a dozen avocados at forty cents apiece. And this is where television comes into it again. They will spend their food money for something like Geritol. Our work is to help them stretch their food dollar—to help them get the most and the best for their money. It isn't easy work. We can't work directly with these people. We represent something they don't understand. They're suspicious and resentful. We have to reach them through their own kind of people. I have five white and three Mexican aides. These are superior women I have been able to attract and interest in our program—women I have trained. They are often neighbors of the people we wish to help. They can go into those homes and talk to the women there—the poor, unhappy teen-age wives who send their kids to school without breakfast. They're down on life. Everything is too much for them. They've given up. But my aides are dedicated and patient. They go in and show them how to plan. They show them how to buy. They show them how hot cereal is cheaper and more nutritious than the cold cereals they hear about on television. They teach them how to cope."

We were driving out through a misty morning countryside—John Henry, who is the Canyon County livestock specialist, and I—in an old Mercury sedan with a mobile weighing chute clanking along behind, to weigh some calves at the farm of a breeder of purebred Red Angus cattle. Henry is forty-one years old—a big, bald, round-faced, slouching man—and he was dressed in the uniform of the stockman: olive-green coveralls and pointed boots. "You know what they say about getting a farm these days," he said. "There's only two ways. Either you inherit it or you marry into it. This old fellow we're going to see, this Layton Todd, he founded the operation, but he and his son are running it together now. What we're going to do this morning is weigh some calves for registry with the Red Angus Association. These calves are all around two hundred days old, and if they're up to standard they should weigh around five hundred pounds. I like working with cattle, but I guess I prefer it this way. My wife and I both like living in town—she plays the organ at the Latter-Day Saints. I grew up on a stock farm. My dad had one of the first Black Angus herds in Idaho. Red Angus is something new. I started milking at the age of six, and at eight I was out there shoveling manure, and when I was old enough for 4-H work I started feeding steers. I saw a lot. I saw my dad knocked down three times and almost killed one day by a dairy bull. Dairy bulls are always inclined to be mean. I got knocked around and cut up pretty good quite a few times myself. And I saw one of my kid friends out baling hay one day, and he slipped and went into the baler. It wired him up like a bale of hay, and the plunger cut him in two. I left the farm when I left home for college. Besides, my dad is still working our place. I got my B.S. in animal husbandry and my M.S. in animal nutrition. This work is exactly right for me. I like to teach. I like to be of service, to make some impact. And everybody knows you. You're a leading citizen." He laughed.

"I mean—Well, gosh, I get my picture in the paper at least once a month."

A sign appeared just ahead on the left: "Black Dust Angus Farms." Henry turned off the road, and we clanked down a lane past a block of cattle corrals tumultuous with bellowing cows and moaning calves. There was a heavy smell of manure and the sour and sickening stink of ensilage. We pulled up at a loading chute halfway down the block. Layton Todd, a red-faced man in coveralls and a big straw hat, was leaning against the chute. Inside the chute, tinkering with a gate, was a pink-cheeked younger man. That was his son, Ze Todd. ("People are always asking about my name," he later told me. "They ought to ask my dad and mother. They saw this movie about Jesse James just before I was born, and Jesse's wife, her name was Zee. My dad and mother had pretty well decided that I was going to be a girl, and that name of Zee appealed to them. And when I turned out to be a boy, they dropped an *e* and gave it to me anyway.") Henry got out and unhitched the weighing chute, and Layton Todd came over and gave him a hand. It was a narrow barred cage on wheels, with a drop gate at one end. Henry and Layton hauled it up alongside one of the corrals. Ze pushed his corral gate open and swung it back to form a pen between the corral and the chute.

"I got three calves here, John," Layton said. "The only trouble is, there's one that's a little too old and two a little too young. Can we adjust? I'd hate to have you turn right around and drive on back to town."

"No problem," Henry said. "A few days don't make all that much difference."

"They're big, too. I tell you, John—these Red Angus calves, they grow faster than the Black. They got that hybrid vigor. All right, Ze. Let's start with that little bull."

A howling, balking, slobbering calf came stumbling through the loading chute. Ze Todd trotted in behind it, swinging a ski pole cut off short for a goad. He prodded it across the makeshift pen and up to the weighing chute. The gate was up, and Henry stood ready to drop it closed. I leaned up over the fence to watch. The calf shied and lurched—and skittered into the fence. The impact bounced me off and sat me down hard on the ground. I heard Henry shout, and Layton call, "Turn him, Ze! He's got himself bassackwards." The calf gave a long, despairing cry. Layton now had a rope around its neck, and, with Ze prodding and Henry waving it on, it dodged, bawling and blubbering, over the threshold and into the chute. The gate dropped with a crash. The little bull stood heaving on the scales. The cows and calves in the corrals all raised their heads and bellowed.

The two other calves were heifers. One was about the size of the little bull and the other was somewhat larger, but they both went almost readily into the weighing chute. The bull was the youngest (one hundred and eighty-seven days) and the lightest (three hundred and forty-five pounds). The larger, and older, of the heifer calves weighed four hundred and ninety-four pounds. It was the last to be weighed. It lumbered back into the corral, back through the staring cows and calves, back to its bellowing mother—drooling, wide-eyed, whimpering.

We stood and watched it go.

"The fuss they make," Henry said. "They act like they think they're beef. If they only knew how lucky they are. They've got the easy life. Nothing to do but breed."

"They got it easier than the breeder," Layton said.

"Dad's right," Ze said. "Breeding cattle isn't like raising, say, chickens. A full-grown purebred bull is a lot of animal. He can service six or seven cows in a day, and it's easy enough to get him started. The trouble is, those cows all look alike to him. So the problem is to get him to service them all—to move him on from No. 1 to No. 2 and from her to No. 3. All you've got is that ring in his nose. It isn't only that bulls can be mean. They're big—they can weigh a ton. I mean, two *thousand* pounds. An animal that big can give you just a little nudge and you'll feel it for a couple of weeks."

"It's like getting nudged by a truck," Henry said.

Samson said, "Which field it is, George?"

George—George Shavers—turned and spat out a wad of tobacco, and lighted a cigarette. "It's both," he said. "But this eighteen acres here is probably the worst. I've only had it just three years, and I've done everything I could, but it don't seem to do no good. I don't know, Merle. The guy that had it before me, he must have let it run down for twenty years."

"I'll bet he did," Samson said. "Well, let's go take a look. You want to take my truck or yours?"

"Mine," Shavers said. "Yours looks too nice and new for these old fields. You know, on top of everything else, I think I've got some gophers coming in. I found a couple of holes the other day. But I wonder what they're going to find to eat in that damn field."

Shavers climbed under the wheel of an old Ford pickup, and Samson and I squeezed in beside him. Samson sat with his tools in his lap—a foot-long tubular soil probe, like a giant apple corer, and a dozen paper soil-sample bags marked "University of Idaho Agricultural Extension Service Soil Testing Laboratory Take Soil Samples Carefully Take a Representative Sample Use Separate Bag for Each Sample." We moved off across the field, jolting against the grain of the furrows.

"There was a young guy down at the café," Shavers said. "He told me manure didn't do no good. I think it was just a theory he had. So I didn't pay no attention."

"I don't know who that young guy was," Samson said. "But he sure wasn't any farmer. The only possible drawback to manure is that it might bring you in some foreign weeds. But I don't call that much of a drawback."

"It ain't to me," Shavers said. "I've already got every damn weed there is."

"O.K., George. Let's pull up here."

We got out in a following cloudburst of dust. It passed, and the air cleared, and I could see the sudden rise of the mountains, twenty miles away. Samson squatted down and worked his probe into the soil as far as it would go. He extracted a core of crumbly earth. He sifted it through his fingers and into a sample bag.

"Sandy loam," he said. "But you've got some clay down deep. I don't like that much. Suppose we move on down the line a couple of hundred yards and try again. Maybe this isn't typical. And, of course, the laboratory may have something else to say."

"I like a sandy loam," Shavers said.

"I do, too," Samson said. "If you water it enough. And often enough. And you need organic matter. I do think you're going to need a lot of manure for this field. Twenty tons to the acre, at least. But I like the tilth. I can see you've worked at cultivation. I don't see all those weeds you were talking about."

"It's cultivation, all right," Shavers said. "It ain't weed killer. I think weed killer is the lazy man's way."

"It's one of his ways," Samson said. "You know what they say. There's two kinds of farmers. There's the one that's got weeds and the one that's got money."

"There's the one that calls the county agent," Shavers said, "and the one that don't bother."

"Right," Samson said. "And there's the one that wants to sleep till seven o'clock in the morning and knock off work at three in the afternoon. He sells his farm to one of the big corporations."

There was the sound of children's voices from a back room at the Canyon County office. I walked down the hall and looked in. On a low platform at one end of the room was a demonstration kitchen, and sitting around a table at the other were ten little girls of eleven or twelve and a pretty young woman in white slacks and a sleeveless blue jersey. Most of the girls had pale-blonde hair, most of them wore dresses, two wore glasses, one was fat, one was a foot taller than the others, and one had an arm in a sling. The woman was Lenora Fields, the other home economist, and this was a 4-H class.

". . . and Charlie," Mrs. Fields was saying, "is Charlie who?"

"*Calcium!*"

"That's right. And Charlie Calcium helps make what?"

"*Teeth and bones!*"

"And where is a good place to get calcium for good teeth and bones?"

"*Milk!*"

"Right. Now, Patty is Patty who?"

"Patty *Protein!*"

"And what does Patty Protein give?"

"*Energy!*"

"That's *right*. And where is a good place to . . ."

Arthur Walz, the area potato-and-onion specialist, and I had an early breakfast at Pollard's Drive-In Cafe. He is a tall, thin man of fifty with sandy-red hair and pale-blue eyes and freckles. We ordered bacon and eggs, and they were served, as usual, with hashed-brown potatoes. Hashed-brown potatoes are the grits of Idaho and the West. We ate to Bill Anderson on the jukebox singing "It Was Time for Me to Move On Anyway," helped ourselves at the cashier's desk to toothpicks and an after-dinner mint, and headed south in a gust of wind and a spurt of rain. Walz opened the glove compartment and got out a pair of sunglasses, and the sky began to clear.

"We've got a name for that," he said. "We call it an Idaho rainstorm. Two or three drops of water and a lot of wind, and then the sun comes out. I think we're going to have another nice hot sunny day for our trip. It's a trip I don't make any oftener than I have to. Owyhee County—the county where we're going—is the biggest county in my area, and it has the fewest people. As a matter of fact, it's one of the biggest counties in the United States. It's almost as big as the state of Massachusetts. But it's very rough country—mostly mountains and high desert. The only real crop is potatoes. There happen to be some very big producers, though, so I have to make a tour every couple of months or so. Those mountains up ahead are the Owyhee Mountains. 'Owyhee' is a phonetic spelling of 'Hawaii.' We had a gold rush here in the early days, back in the eighteen-sixties, and it seems that a lot of prospectors were Hawaiians. One big bunch of them had the misfortune to get massacred by the Indians. So the other prospectors starting calling the place where it happened Owyhee."

We crossed the Snake River at the village of Marsing.

Marsing was the beginning of Owyhee County. We stopped there for gas and to pick up the Owyhee County agent—a calm, square-built, gray-haired man named Glenn Bodily—and then continued south. It was a different countryside on this side of the river. The fertile Canyon County flats gave way to stony sagebrush hills and salt-grass hollows and occasional towering purple buttes. The river wound among the hills, and there were river meadows here and there, sometimes with a cow or two grazing in them. The air was hot and dry, and the sky was a hazy blue. A grove of trees appeared, like a mirage, ahead.

"That's Given's Hot Springs," Bodily said. "It used to be a famous resort."

"It was nice," Walz said. "People used to drive all the way down from Caldwell for a picnic in the shade of those old locust trees. Now all they want to do is stay at home with the air-conditioning on and watch the television."

The wilderness returned. Walz touched his lips with a protective salve, and pointed to a big falling-down frame building on the riverbank a mile or two away. "And there's a short history of Owyhee County," he said. "That started out as an Indian fort. Then they turned it into a ferry house. Then it was somebody's barn. Now it's nothing."

The road swung away from the river. We began to climb through an even wilder, even emptier countryside. And then, on a hilltop far ahead, a cluster of buildings came into view. A filling-station café. A one-story yellow brick building with a flagpole in front. Half a dozen houses. We passed a sign: "Murphy, Ida. Home of All-Girl Rodeo." We pulled off the road and into the filling station. A plump blonde girl in jeans and boots watched us from a bench at the door of the café.

"Murphy is our Owyhee County seat," Bodily said. "And that is all it is. They put the seat here in the early days because this is more or less the middle of the county. It's about halfway between the two settled areas. That brick building there is a courthouse. There's nothing else but that and this and a post office. Well, let's go have us a cup of coffee." He opened the door. "Hello, Teddy."

"Hi, there," the girl said.

"Teddy," Walz said. "What's the population here? About thirty?"

"Oh, no," she said. "I think it's up around seventy. But if you really want to know I'll find out. I'll count it."

We drank our scalding, watery coffee at the counter. The only other customers were two old men with stubbly sunken cheeks, wearing faded overalls and big hats and silently drinking beer. Behind the counter was a fat woman with a pile of bright-red hair. Teddy was waiting for us when we came out.

"I was wrong," she said. "It isn't seventy—it's only fifty-five. I guess a couple of families must have moved away."

After Murphy, the road began to worsen. There were potholes in the asphalt, and patches of cobblestone gravel.

The mountains were edging closer. They rose higher and higher, with many thrusting peaks, but the slopes were green and gently rolling. "I've been chukar hunting all through there," Walz said. "Appearances are deceiving. It looks easy from here. But when you get up close—when you really get up in there—it's rough. You climb and climb and climb, and then you happen to stop and look back. You know you've been working, but when you look back down at all those shelves and rockslides, it scares you. It's a shock to see what you've been climbing through. And way, way down there is a tiny little speck, and you realize: My God, it's my car."

"This is all rough country in here," Bodily said. "It's pretty close to desolation. Some of Owyhee County is like Canyon County—all it needs is water. But this is different. The soil is different. Sagebrush is a good indicator of topsoil. Its size and abundance tell you something. But you don't see any sage along here. There's nothing but shad scale and rabbit brush. That white dust you see out there is bentonite clay. That's your soil, and it's almost impervious to water."

"They used to use bentonite to seal their irrigation ditches," Walz said. "It's almost as tight as cement. Bentonite is real bad news to farmers."

"You bet it is," Bodily said. "And a lot of farmers have had to find that out the hard way. I've seen them trying to plow it. But you know something, Art? That fork back there—I'm not too sure we're on the right road. You can get lost in this damn country."

"Not really," Walz said. "Somebody's bound to come along and find you in a day or two."

The road ran on through the featureless flats. There was nothing to see but the mountains and an occasional sculptured butte. The road turned and dipped and twisted down a hill. We crossed a little bridge with a trickle of creek below. Beyond the bridge were three or four houses. Then a ramshackle Pepsi-Cola store. Then a big stone Catholic church in a grove of poplar trees. Bodily gave a grunt and sat back.

"O.K., Art," he said. "We're in Oreana. But I haven't been down through here in quite some while."

"Oreana is one of our Basque colonies," Walz said. "They used to run sheep in here, but now it's mostly cattle. I don't know how they're making out."

"They do all right," Bodily said. "There's pretty good grazing on this side of the creek. They're interesting people. I remember a fellow just south of here who had a little stock operation. I came down with a specialist, and we looked over his range and his water and all the rest, and we worked out a nice expansion program for him. We were there for most of a day. And then he shook his head. 'I don't know,' he said. 'I think I'm happier the way I am.'"

Walz had two afternoon appointments. Both were with big potato growers whose holdings were on the high sagebrush plains beyond Oreana. We stopped on the way for a sandwich at the Black Sands Cafe, in a tourist camp on the shore of a storage lake at the confluence of the Snake and one of its tributary rivers. The lake was a strange sight. Its waters were blue and sparkling in the sun, but the shores were arid desert. There were no trees, no greenery of shrub or grass. The gray, dusty desert brush ran down to the beach banks, down to the edge of the water. The only sign of life was six or seven coots floating at the mouth of a marshy cove.

After the lake, the potato fields—high and hot and windswept—had a look that was almost lush. The first of the farms was a corporate enterprise with some five thousand acres under cultivation. "We're running a little planting experiment here," Walz said. "Potato plants are usually grown about nine inches apart. We're trying them here at six inches. This is a big operation, with a big production, but they want to make it even bigger. That's why they're big." He and Bodily and a section lessee spent half an hour together—strolling along an endless field, stopping and talking, pointing and moving slowly on, nodding and frowning and tracing boot-toe patterns in the dust. I joined them for a while, and then went back to the shade of the car. The other farm was a two-thousand-acre fraction of a family operation. Walz was there to meet a group of salesmen and test two types of humidifiers for use in a new potato-storage barn. I watched the tests with one of the family, a polite young man named Blaine Mecham. He had on the usual battered boots and an imitation-leopard-skin cap. "No," he said. "I went to Utah State. My people are Latter-Day Saints. And I didn't go to ag school. After all, I was raised on a farm. I thought I'd do better to learn something I didn't already know. I majored in sociology, and my minor was ag economics. Then I worked for a year for the Bank of America in Fresno. Then I was ready to come back home and go to work. I hardly ever do any physical work myself. But I'm always here. I drive around and keep the men going. The market doesn't matter too much to us. We don't grow baking potatoes in this area. That's all done in the eastern part of the state, where it's high and cool. Our potatoes here grow too big for baking. We sell our crop by contract to the processor. If you've ever eaten any frozen French fries, you've probably eaten some of our potatoes. No, we don't live up here. We live in town—in Mountain Home."

We drove back to Marsing through the last heavy heat of the desert afternoon. "I like to see a good operation," Walz said. "And we've seen a couple today. They aren't as common as some people like to think. The day of the hick is long gone. Farming is a real profession now. It demands a lot of a man. I've never seen a good farmer who wasn't above average in intelligence. He has to know how to handle men, he has to be able to plan, and he has to be able to manage land—he has to understand the land. I've known potato growers to get a yield of three hundred and fifty hundredweight to the acre and still go belly up. They were thinking yield when they should have been thinking quality. Quality is work. You don't get quality by sitting around the café drinking coffee at ten o'clock in the morning. You have to live with the crop. That's one thing that hasn't changed. The best fertilizer is still the grower's shadow. We try to teach them that."

It was almost six o'clock when we dropped Bodily off at his office. The sun was low, and the air was beginning to cool. We crossed the river and climbed up through darkening orchards to the flats. The burgeoning fields began—mint and onions and alfalfa and beets and corn and beans—and there was a smell of blossomy sweetness. It was strange to think that this had once been a desert as forbidding as much of Owyhee County. I had a curious feeling that I had spent the day in the past. Owyhee County was a survival of the original Idaho. I had been given a glimpse of what Washington Irving saw for days on end when he passed this way in 1810. "It is a land," he wrote in *Astoria*, his account of that journey, "where no man permanently resides; a vast uninhabited solitude, with precipitous cliffs and yawning ravines, looking like the ruins of a world; vast desert tracts that must ever defy cultivation and interpose dreary and thirsty wilds between the habitations of man."

Walz said, "Are you in a big hurry to get back to town?"

"Not particularly," I said. "Why?"

"I want to make a little detour for a minute."

He turned off the highway and down a dim gravel road. We drove slowly along for about a mile and pulled up at a twilit potato field. Walz opened his door and got out.

"I'll be right back," he said. "There's something I . . ."

He hopped across an irrigation ditch and climbed the bank and walked out to the edge of the field. I watched him standing there in the gathering dusk with his hands on his hips, looking down the long, sprouting rows. He came back and got under the wheel and started the engine.

"Something wrong?" I said.

"Wrong?" he said. "Oh, no. I just wanted to see— This field belongs to a fellow I've been working with. He had a little problem, and I've been a little worried. So I thought I'd just stop by and see. But it looks real nice, doesn't it? I think we're going to do all right."

A Peaceable Town

Stapleton, where I lived for a month in the spring of 1970, is a crossroads county seat in the Sand Hills country of western Nebraska. It was founded in 1912, and it has a population of three hundred and three. The Sand Hills are grassy dunes. They are great, oceanic waves of sand with a carpeting of the rich native grass that nourished the buffalo—sand bluestem, prairie sand reed, sand love-grass, switch grass, needle and thread. Briefly green in the short prairie spring, then brown and dry and blowing in the perpetual prairie wind, the Sand Hills form the largest natural cattle range in the United States. They cover all or much of twenty Nebraska counties. One of these, Cherry County, is bigger than Connecticut and Rhode Island combined. Logan County, of which Staple-ton is the seat, is the smallest of the Sand Hills counties. It is roughly twice the size of Cape Cod. The Sand Hills grasslands are the quiddity of Stapleton. They surround and contain and sustain it. They also isolate it. Stapleton is the only town in Logan County. Its nearest neighbor is the village of Arnold (pop. 755), twenty miles away to the east, in Custer County. North Platte (pop. 19,287), the metropolis of western Nebraska, is twenty-nine miles to the south. Thedford (pop. 293) is thirty-six miles to the north, and a roadside hamlet called Tryon (pop. 166) is twenty-seven miles to the west. There is nothing be-tween Stapleton and its neighbors—nothing at all. No roadhouses, no drive-ins, not even a filling station. There is only the long, empty highway and the range. Sometimes, in the distance, one can see a clump of trees and a windmill and a ranch house. The population of rural Logan County—that is, the county exclusive of Stapleton—is six hundred and ninety-one.

Stapleton is linked to its neighbors by two highways. They are U.S. Highway 83, the main north-and-south route in the area, and Nebraska Highway 92, running east and west. Both are single-lane blacktop highways, and they intersect at a right-angle crossing about half a mile east of the village. Stapleton stands in a windbreak grove of cottonwoods and Chinese elms, and can be only glimpsed from the intersection. Except in winter, when the leaves are down, travelers often pass it unawares. Highway 92 runs through the middle of Stapleton and is one of its two main streets, but Stapleton is not a highway village. It was differently designed. It was laid out as a railroad town. Stapleton came into being (on a section—or square mile—of land provided by two pioneer cattlemen) as the terminus of a branch line of the Union Pacific Railroad, and its second main street is Main Street, which runs north and south. Main Street is eighty feet wide and half a mile long, and it runs from one end of town to the other. It begins at the yellow clapboard Union Pacific Depot, at the north end, and it ends at the red brick Stapleton Consolidated School. There is a parade on Main Street every weekday morning (weather permitting) during the school year. This is part of the training of the Stapleton High School Band. The band marches—flags flying and drum majorettes strutting—out from the school and up to the depot and back. People come out of the Main Street stores and offices and stand and watch it go by.

Stapleton has always been a village. It has never been much larger than it is today. Once, around 1930, its population climbed as high as five hundred and one. The village is now a little smaller than it was at the time of the First World War. But Stapleton has the look of a town—an urban look. There are no wandering, cowpath streets, no straggle out along the highway. It is plotted in the urban gridiron pattern, and its limits are clearly defined. The backyards of the outermost houses all end at a barbed-wire fence, and beyond the fence is the range. Stapleton has several urban amenities. It has a municipal park with a tennis court and picnic ovens and picnic tables and benches. It maintains the county ambulance (the nearest hospitals are St. Mary's Hospital and Memorial Hospital, in North Platte), and the drivers, members of the fire department, are trained in first aid. It has a municipal waterworks and a municipal sewer system. Its telephone system is fully automatic, and the lines are laid underground. Most of the streets are lighted and paved, and the paved streets all have sidewalks. The streets are named in the functional urban fashion. The north-south streets—the streets that parallel Main Street—are named for the letters of the alphabet. There are ten of these streets—A Street through J Street. (Main Street runs between F and G.) The other streets are numbered. They run from First Street, at the depot, to Sixth Street, at the school. Highway 92 is known formally as Third Street. There are, however, no street signs in Stapleton, and (except for Main Street) the street names are never used. The intersection of Main Street and Highway 92 is usually called the Corner.

Most Stapletonians are born in a North Platte hospital, and almost all of them are buried in one or another of three Logan County cemeteries—McCain, St. John's, and Loup Valley. Loup Valley Cemetery is the smallest and most remote. It lies in a fold in the range about ten miles west of Stapleton, on the road to Tryon. St. John's, a Roman Catholic cemetery that was consecrated in 1915, and McCain are both just east of town, on the road that leads to Arnold. McCain is the largest of the three cemeteries, and by far the oldest. It was established (as the gift of the widow of a pioneer named Robert McCain) in 1884, and it occupies four acres on a hilltop planted with bushy box elders and big, spreading cedars. It offers a commanding view of the surrounding countryside, and also of the past. A majority of the early settlers (and the founders of the established local families) are buried there: Miller, Burnside, Hartzell, Clark, Wheeler, Smith, Wells, Bay, Perry, Erickson, Abrams, Joedeman, Salisbury, Loudon. Many of the pioneers were veterans of the Civil War, all having served with the Union Army. The notations on their headstones are geographically descriptive: "Co. C, 9 Ohio Cavalry"; "Co. A, 81 Pa. Infantry"; "Co. H, 71 N.Y. Infantry"; "10 Indiana Cav."; "Co. F, 86 Ill. Inf."; "Co. D, 1st Iowa Cavalry"; "Co. E, 5th Iowa Infantry."

Except for an elaborate white marble shaft commemorating Robert McCain, and one or two other monumental monuments, the headstones are modest tablets. A few are inscribed with conventional pieties ("Though thou art done, fond mem'ry clings to thee"), but most of them carry only a name and a date. The given names of the men are equally conventional: Joseph, William, Richard, John, Edward. The given names of the women at McCain, and also at Loup Valley (though not, of course, at St. John's), are more imaginative. Some of them are wildly so: Melita, Alvirda, Glenola, Vernie Lynn, Tressa, Verla, Idara, Delma, Velna, Zetta, Uhleen, Berdie, Zella, Lesta, Verga, Lenna, Jacobina, Dalorus, Tilitha, Caline, Mayden, Sedona, Orpha, Doralie, Urah. These names are not, as I at first supposed, the fancies of a vanished generation. Such names are still popular in Stapleton. A high-school senior I met is named Vaneta. One of her classmates is named Wilda. A first grader, about whom I read, is named Jeanna. A second grader is named Tena. There is a sixth grader named Kerri. And the first name of Mrs. Robert A. Perry, the wife of a prominent Logan County rancher, is Alta May.

Practically everybody in Stapleton lives on the south side of town. There are only five families on the north side of the highway. The churches—Presbyterian, Catholic, and Assembly of God—are all in the residential area. The First Presbyterian Church—the largest and oldest of the Stapleton churches—and the fundamentalist Assembly of God are both on Main Street, south of the Corner, and St. John's Catholic Church is a block to the west. There is plenty of space in Stapleton (there are vacant lots on every block), but most of the houses are built on fifty-foot plots. "The Sand Hills is a big country," James Morey, a farmer who now lives in town, told me. "If you ever homesteaded up on the Dismal River, like I did, you'd know what I'm talking about. People like company. They like to have close neighbors." Some of the houses are brick, some are asbestos shingle, and some are clapboard painted white, but they are otherwise much alike. The usual house has one story, with a little stepped stoop and a low-pitched pyramidal roof. The chairman of the Board of Trustees, the governing body of Stapleton—a retired (and reputedly well-to-do) merchant and landowner named John Beckius—lives in such a house, and so does Mrs. Vivian Nelson, a laundress. The biggest house in town is the Catholic rectory. Most of the houses have flower and vegetable gardens, and the lawns are often strangely ornamented. Some people move old, axe-handled back-yard pumps around to the front and paint them in bright colors. Many people cut openings in plastic Clorox bottles and hang them up as houses for purple martins. People also paint old coffeepots and teakettles and hang them in groups from poles and plant them with geraniums and petunias and marigolds. The garage of one house has a garden of cabbage-size pink roses and giant blue delphiniums painted on an outside wall. "That wall goes back to our painting fad," Mrs. Earl Glandon, an amateur artist and the wife of a former postmaster, told me. "A professional artist came to town for a while and gave painting lessons, and there were about fourteen ladies that joined the class. One of the ladies painted that garage wall. Another lady, a widow lady, heard about a famous old sod house out south of town somewhere, and she went there and painted a picture of it, and a little later the man who owned the sod house asked her about the picture, and she invited him over to see it, and he came and they got friendly and he married her. He moved her into his sod house, and the first thing she did was to paint it. She painted wisteria around the door and morning-glories climbing up the walls of the house. It was like that garage. She made it look more cheerful."

The main business block in Stapleton is Main Street just north of the Corner. It is a sunbaked block in summer —the only block in Stapleton without a twilit canopy of trees—but the sidewalks in front of some of the buildings are shaded by metal awnings. Most of the buildings on the block are one-story buildings of red or yellow brick. About half of them have high false fronts. There are two vacant buildings on the block. One is an old store full of broken fixtures. The other is a boarded-up movie house. It went out of business in 1955, but there is a painted-over name still visible on the façade: "The New Theater." The block contains six stores. Three of them are grocery stores (Black's Thriftway Grocery, Denny's Market, and Ewoldt's Grocery & Locker), and there is a hardware store (Hanna's Supply), a feed store (Miller Ranch Supply), and a farm-equipment store (Salisbury Implement Company). All of them are more or less general stores. Ewoldt's is almost a department store. It occupies three rooms on the ground floor of a two-story building that was once the Hildenbrandt Hotel (there are twenty-one numbered rooms, including a bridal suite, on the second floor), and it sells—along with meats and groceries—drugs, cosmetics, notions, toys, memorial wreaths, school supplies, work clothes, boots, big hats, and ice. The other business buildings on the block are a laundromat (Bud's Holiday Laundry), a bowling alley (Bronco Bowl), the Stapleton *Enterprise* (a weekly paper), and the Bank of Stapleton. There is also a two-story (with a false front) Masonic Temple, and an American Legion Post. The bank is on the northwest corner of the Corner, and it is the most imposing building on the block. It is a square brick building with ornamental cornices and glass-brick windows and a high, pedimented roof. Along the highway side is a two-rail iron-pipe railing. On Saturday afternoons, there are usually a couple of cowboys sitting there with their heels hooked over the bottom rail and their hats tipped down on their noses.

The Stapleton Post Office, a red brick building that somewhat resembles the bank, is on the southwest corner of the Corner. Across Main Street from the post office is Chesley's Barber Shop. "I've only got one complaint," Everette C. Chesley, the barber, told me. "It isn't about long hair. The kids around here don't wear their hair what I would call short, but they do come in and get hair-cuts. My complaint is shaves. I used to shave maybe fifteen fellows of a Saturday. The last time I shaved a fellow was an old man two months ago. I might as well get rid of my razors. A razor is like an arm or a leg. It goes dead unless you use it." Next door to the barbershop is the Logan County Courthouse. The courthouse was built in 1963 and is the newest building in Stapleton. It is an L-shaped building faced with polished pink granite, with a flagpole in front and a parking lot and an acre of well-kept lawn. There is a little cluster of businesses up around the depot. The office and storage bins of the Stapleton Mill & Elevator Co. are there, and a feed lot, and two lumberyards—the S. A. Foster Lumber Company and the Greenslit Lumber Company. Their yards are stacked with big round metal water troughs and creosoted fence posts and spools of barbed wire. (In Stapleton, as everywhere else west of Pittsburgh, barbed wire is "bob wire.") Except for two living-room beauty parlors—one (Dotti's Beauty Salon) on the west side of town and the other (Beauty Shop) in a house near the school—the other Stapleton businesses are all situated on the highway. Just west of the Corner are a beer bar and liquor store (Wagon Wheel Tavern) and a Rural Electrification Administration garage. East of the Corner are a farm-equipment store (Magnuson Implement Company), two filling stations (East Side Skelly Service and A. A. Gulf Service), the fire station, and the Whiteway Cafe & Motel.

"My wife and I took over the newspaper in 1960," Arthur French, the publisher of the *Enterprise*, told me.

"We came over from Tryon. Tryon is pretty little, and it's also pretty staid. Stapleton is more like a town. When we first arrived here, there were maybe a few more business places than there are now. There was another café and a drugstore. But they were mostly run by older people with their money down deep in their pockets. They were just setting there. Now all the stores have younger people in charge. Dick Black at the Thriftway and Elwin Miller at the Ranch Supply and Dick Kramer at the Skelly station, they're just in their twenties, and Alfred Ewoldt isn't very much older. Neither is Dean Hanna, at the Gulf station. I'm still under forty myself. Even Ed Burnham—Edwin H. Burnham, the president of the bank and I guess you could say our leading citizen. He has the insurance agency there at the bank and he owns a lot of property and he has a big interest in the elevator and he's building himself a new fifty-thousand-dollar home out east of town. Even Ed is only about fifty. Ed believes in Stapleton, and he'll put up money to prove it. Ed gave me my start here with a very generous loan. We've also got a real nice Chamber of Commerce, with thirty-five members, and I think we've got a future. Our only problem is getting help. I could use another man in our printshop, and I had a fellow lined up down in the Platte. He drove up with his wife one day. They made a couple of passes around town and then came into the shop and the wife said, 'I didn't see the shopping center. Where is it?' I said we didn't have a shopping center here. 'Let's go,' she said."

The name of Edwin H. Burnham is often heard in Stapleton. He is not always in residence there (during my stay he was sojourning at a hunting lodge he has in Canada), but his presence is constantly felt. "Our banker is the pleasantest man you ever saw," Charles V. Greenslit, the owner of the lumberyard that bears his name, told me. "Hail fellow well met. Always smiling. Generous. Gave our village an ambulance. Gives to all the churches. Our old banker—the man who brought Ed Burnham here—he was just the opposite. He was conservative. He was the kind of banker who wouldn't think of making a loan unless you hardly needed the money. Burnham's happy to help anybody. And he's done well for himself. Real well. Everything he touches turns to money. I sometimes wonder how he does it. He's never here. But he's building himself a sixty-thousand-dollar home out east of town. So maybe he's planning to settle down." Everybody seems to think well of Burnham. "Ed Burnham is a real asset," Leslie M. Bay, the county judge, told me. "When we were getting ready to build the new courthouse, he got us a big bond break. He bid our building bonds down to three per cent, and then stepped back and let somebody else bid them in at two point eighty-five per cent. One of our problems here is housing. Ed won't let a house fall down. He'll fix it up and put it back to work. He's always finding an old house out in the county somewhere and moving it into town. Right now, he's building himself a nice new home on some land he owns out east of here. I understand it's costing him in the neighborhood of seventy-five thousand dollars. Of course, Ed has improved himself. He's made a lot of money. But you'd never know he had a dime. He's as common as an old shoe. He'd just as soon set down and drink a bottle of beer as not. Wherever he's at, that's what he is. Ed's at home anywhere. He's a rancher out at your ranch. In Rome, he's a Roman."

The Whiteway was my home in Stapleton. I had a room (with a big springy bed and a rocking chair and a table) in the Motel, and I took my meals at the Cafe. The Cafe occupies the front end of a long, narrow, shingle-sided building with a low, overhanging roof all around and a gravelly unpaved parking lot on three sides. The Motel is in back, behind the kitchen, and overlooks a chicken yard patrolled by three excitable roosters. It consists of five rooms (with baths) and the apartment of the manager. The Whiteway is owned by a woman in Hooker County, and it is leased from her by a Logan County farmer named James Wonch. (Wonch is a powerful man with a shaven head and dark-brown eyes. I had been in Stapleton about a week before I met him, and I was strangely struck by his appearance. There was something unusual about his looks that I couldn't quite identify. I thought at first that it must be his shaven head—and then I realized. The unusual thing was his eyes. Almost everybody in Stapleton—everybody but Wonch and one or two others—has blue eyes.) The manager of the Whiteway is a plump, pretty, white-haired widow (with blue eyes) named Clarice Olson, and she also does most of the cooking and all of the baking at the Cafe. "I open up at about six-thirty, and we close at night when the last customer gets up and leaves," Mrs. Olson told me. "That's usually around ten o'clock. Our people come in for breakfast, for second breakfast, for midmorning coffee, for noon dinner, for afternoon coffee, for supper, and for evening coffee. There's usually somebody waiting when I open up in the morning. Most of the time, it's Red Black. Red and his wife both work for the county. He's a road grader, and she cleans at the courthouse. Red drives her to work and then comes around for his coffee. Half the time, he opens the door for me. Then he sits and watches me get my baking started. I bake two dozen cinnamon rolls every morning, and about a half a dozen pies. Always apple, always cherry, and either lemon or chocolate meringue. Sometimes I make a few doughnuts. Then I get dinner started. My first dinner customer is Vera Gragg, one of the tellers at the bank. She comes in at eleven-thirty on the dot. They're my most regular customers—Vera and Red Black." Mrs. Olson's daughter, a divorcée named LaDonna Wisdom, is the regular Cafe waitress, and a young girl named Grace Young helps out when needed. For much of my stay, I was the only traveler at the Motel, but the Cafe was almost always crowded. There were always a couple of cars pulled up in front (nobody in Stapleton ever walks anywhere), and usually a dusty pickup truck from one of the farms or ranches. The Cafe is the social center of Stapleton. Almost everybody in town drops in at some time almost every day. One Sunday afternoon, I counted a dozen cars parked there. Three of them were Cadillacs.

The Cafe is a clean and comfortable café. It is warm in cold weather and icily air-conditioned in summer, and the three outer walls are windows. There are six cream-and-gold Formica tables around the window walls, and a counter with five stools across the back. A door at one end of the counter opens into a private dining room that will accommodate about twenty diners. The Chamber of Commerce holds its monthly dinner meetings there. There is a soda fountain behind the counter (with a display of candy bars and chewing gum and foil-wrapped bandoliers of Alka-Seltzer), but the cooking is all done in the kitchen. There is a jukebox the size of an organ near the dining-room door, with an automated repertoire of "Lonesome Highway" and "Sugar Shack" and a hundred other country-and-Western tunes. There are a Coca-Cola machine and a Dr. Pepper machine and a cigarette machine. There is a bulletin board on the wall near the jukebox with a calendar ("Compliments Central Nebraska Commission Co., Broken Bow, Nebr., Cattle Sale Every Saturday") and an assortment of bulletins ("Wanted Write-in Votes for Joe Klosen"; "Midwest Breeders Cooperative: Beef & Dairy Semen, Liquid Nitrogen, A-I Supplies"; "The Last Pages—for booking, call Steve Myers, Bill Dolan, Doug Wallace, N. Platte"; "Bull Sale, Ogallala Sale Barn, Ogallala, Nebr. 39 Angus, 2 Charolais, 45 Herefords, 5 Shorthorns") and a motto ("No Man Is Good Enough to Govern Another Without the Other's Consent"). There is a

blackboard menu on the wall behind the counter with one permanent entry: "Roast Beef, $1.40." Other entries that appear on the board from time to time are "Scalloped Potatoes & Ham, $1.25" and "Salmon Loaf, $1.25." The roast beef is pot roast. Steak is never listed on the menu but it is always available, and it is always cut thin and always chicken-fried. There is a sign near the blackboard: "Margarine Served Here." The bread is Rainbo Bread.

One rainy morning, I lingered over breakfast at the Cafe. I sat at a window table and ate fried eggs and thick pancakes and watched the cars pull in and out and the customers come and go. Several of the cars had little decal American flags on the windows, and one had a bumper sticker: "Trust in Christ." Some sparrows were nesting under the eaves of the Cafe, and they flew from car to car, feeding on the insects shattered on the radiator grilles. I knew some of the customers by name and most of the others by sight. There were three R.E.A. technicians in cowboy hats and boots. There was Alfred Ewoldt in cowboy boots and a hunting cap. There was a young cowboy in a sweatshirt with lettering across the back: ". . . and a Follower of Women." There was an elderly farmer in bib overalls matching double or nothing for coffee with the waitress, LaDonna Wisdom. There was the county judge, Judge Bay, with a lump of snuff under his lower lip, and Mrs. Thomas Mahoney, the village clerk and the wife of a Union Pacific conductor. There were two school-bus drivers (of a total of nine)—Mrs. Beverly Lehmkuhler, a widow, and Mrs. Norman Yardley, the wife of the high-school principal—eating a second breakfast; they rise early to circle the county and bring the students in to school. There was Mrs. Noma Wells, the widow of a merchant and landowner, who spends much of her time driving around town in a saffron-yellow Cadillac. (Her car is one of five Cadillacs in Stapleton, and there are also three new Lincoln Continentals.) There was a thin girl in jeans and a T-shirt. There was James Wonch. There was a tall, stooped, flat-bellied cowboy in a rodeo shirt with the sleeves cut off at the shoulders. There was James Morey, the former Dismal River homesteader, with an old black hat on the back of his head, talking to the other waitress, Grace Young. I sat and looked and listened.

JAMES MOREY: How about you and me having a date sometime?

GRACE YOUNG: I don't go out with old whiskery men.

JAMES MOREY: I could shave. But have I got a chance? I ain't going to shave in the middle of the week unless there's at least a chance.

MRS. LEHMKUHLER: The first one I picked up this morning brought me an apple. And another one gave me some fudge. They're going to get me fat.

JAMES WONCH: It's a funny thing. My dad used to walk to school. I rode a horse. But all my kids have to do is stand and wait for the bus.

LaDONNA WISDOM: One week, I cut down eating and I gained five pounds. When I stepped on the scales, I was real disgusted. So I went back to eating.

ELDERLY FARMER: I'll match you for one of them rolls.

R.E.A. MAN: Marijuana?

SECOND R.E.A. MAN: They call it pot. It looks like it's moving this way. They say the kids have got it at Broken Bow.

THIRD R.E.A. MAN: We used to call it Mary Jane.

MRS. MAHONEY: I don't know about the Platte. But they have never had to draft a boy from here. Or from Tryon. Or from Arnold, for that matter.

GIRL IN THE T-SHIRT: No, I've just got the two. But I was married at fifteen and I'm only eighteen now and I'm not going to have no more. For a while, anyway. I will say this. I never had no trouble having any of my kids. The girl next to me the last time, she had a Caesarean. My second baby, he's ten months now, but a couple of months ago he couldn't sit up or anything. He had the rickets. They started giving him lots of vitamins, and now he can sit and everything real good.

MRS. WELLS: I'm washing at Bud's this morning, so while I'm working I thought I'd have some coffee.

MRS. MAHONEY: LaDonna, I came away this morning without any matches. Have you got some?

LaDonna Wisdom: Here—can you catch?

Mrs. Mahoney: I catch real good. When you've got a boy in the Boy Scouts working on merit badges, you can do a lot of things. I can tie knots and make a fire and talk in Morse code. I can do a hundred things I never wanted to do.

Mrs. Yardley: Be glad you haven't got a daughter. Mine has been practicing for the 4-H cake demonstration, and she ended up in the kitchen last Saturday with eighteen sponge cakes.

Judge Bay: It don't blow every day, but then it blows twice the next day to make up for it.

Mrs. Mahoney: . . . sewing on Sunday. My mother would have said that I'll never get to Heaven until I stop and take those stitches out with my nose. She also used to say that you haven't learned to sew until you've learned to rip.

The cowboy in the sleeveless shirt got up to go, and stopped and looked at me, and then came over. "Excuse me," he said. "But you look mighty familiar to me. I wonder haven't I seen you someplace before. Where are you from?"

I told him that I lived in New York.

"That could be it," he said. "I could have seen you there. I used to travel—before and after the service. My feet have been on every soil in the continental United States and the world. Except only Russia. I used to speak fourteen different languages, but I didn't keep it up. Now I've only got one. Well, *choco-chuco-mungo-mango-boola-mack.*"

"What?" I said.

"That's Indian for 'see you later,'" he said.

I was ready to leave, too. I pushed back my chair and put a tip on the table ("You don't have to do that every time," LaDonna said), and paid my bill, and followed the cowboy out. My breakfast, including orange juice and coffee, cost sixty cents.

The Cafe is not exclusively an adult gathering place. It also serves as the corner drugstore for the teen-age boys of Stapleton. There are a few boys hanging around nearly every evening, but their big night there is Friday night. They drift up after supper in their dress-up clothes—clean, faded bluejeans, two-toned, high-heeled boots with fancy stitching, big hats (felt in winter, straw in summer), and brightly patterned shirts with double pockets and snaps for buttons. Most of the boys have cars (drivers are licensed at sixteen in Nebraska), and they lean against the parked cars in front of the Cafe and kick gravel and wrestle and yell to each other ("Hey, Larry—where's Kramer and those guys?") and stomp inside and play the jukebox and get Cokes and come shoving out and trade arm punches, and the boys with dates drive up and the others flock around and make jokes ("Hey, is that a new shirt, or is that a new shirt?"), and the girls in the cars laugh and comb their hair and shriek back and forth, and every now and then a car with a couple in it will start up abruptly ("Watch him lay some rubber now. He's put fifty thousand miles on those tires and half of it is just in starts") and take off down the highway and after a while come roaring back and park again and sit and then suddenly charge off once more, with the radio thumping and twanging, and this time the car will head out toward U.S. 83 and Arnold, or west toward Tryon, and pretty soon all the couples are gone and the jukebox stops and the Cafe lights go out, and then the car doors begin to slam and the engines race and the remaining cars move off and up to the depot and down past the school and home.

The courthouse is the office building of Stapleton. It houses around a dozen village, county, state, and federal offices. The village clerk and the village marshal; the county clerk, the county treasurer, the county (or probate) judge, the county welfare director, the county Board of Commissioners (the executive body concerned with taxes, roads, budgets, assessments), and the county sheriff; the state Agricultural Extension Service representative (or county agent); and two agencies of the United States Department of Agriculture—all have offices there. The building also houses a courtroom (with a jury room and chambers for the visiting district judge at his quarterly sessions), a jail (with two cells), a local-history museum, and a public library.

The museum is an accretion of odds and ends (a wooden lemon press, an 1807 edition of the Bible, two shaving mugs, a pair of "Driving Gloves worn by E. R. Smith when he drove the second car in Logan County in 1907," a blue glass ball stamped "Harden's Hand Grenade Fire Extinguisher Pat. 1871") arranged in a case in the courtroom foyer, but the library is a substantial one. It has an annual budget for books of five hundred dollars, and an accessible collection of some thirty-four thousand books, including a shelf of standard Nebraska authors— Willa Cather, Mari Sandoz, John G. Neihardt, Bess Streeter Aldrich. It is an active library, and the children are introduced to it at an early age through a weekly story hour conducted by volunteer readers. Some women drive in with their children from distant ranches for the weekly reading. ("This is a real conservative community," Charles Hunnel, the superintendent of the Stapleton school, told me. "The people here believe very highly in education. Our annual budget at the school is over two hundred thousand dollars. That's almost half the total tax income of the county. We have a very high educational level. More than half of our high-school graduates go on to college, and we have practically no dropouts. In my seven years in this job, we've had just two—two girls dropped out to get married. We haven't produced any geniuses. It isn't an intellectual community. But there's a real respect for learning.") The librarian is a widow named Florence L. Brown. Mrs. Brown is also something of a local historian. "People are always asking me where Stapleton got its name," she told me. "Well, I finally found out. I found an editorial in a copy of the *Enterprise* for October 17, 1912, that explained everything. I made a copy for the library, and here it is. Sit down and read it." It read:

> Mr. D. C. Stapleton has for the past thirty years felt an abiding interest and faith in the future of central western Nebraska, and while his larger interests have called him abroad for the greater part of the time, for several years past, he has never lost sight of the fact that out here in Nebraska was the place of all the rest that he could call "home," for it was here he homesteaded in the year 1884 and it was in recognition of his high ideals of what western Nebraska ought to be and do, and his constant efforts toward that goal that this city was named "Stapleton" in his honor.

There is no crime in Stapleton. People leave the keys in their cars and the doors of their houses unlocked. Don Vetter, the village marshal, wears a policeman's blue cap, but he is only nominally a peace officer. His main job is operating the water plant, the sewage plant, and the village dump. Law and order is formally represented in Stapleton by the Logan County sheriff. The sheriff is a big, comfortable man of sixty-two with a star on his shirt and a smile on his face and a revolver in a drawer of his desk. His name is Arthur Wiley, and he has been sheriff since 1954. "Order is no problem here," he told me. "This is a peaceable town. Nobody crowds anybody. There's plenty of leeway. A man has got the freedom to go out and holler if he wants to. Law is what I'm mostly concerned with. I mean summonses and traffic offenses and things like that. No local boy has ever got in serious trouble in my time in office. Once in a while, I break up a fight at the bar. That's usually in August, when we have our fair and rodeo and some cowboy pours a glass of beer down some other guy's neck. We've never in history had a murder here. I did get shot up once. A couple of kids started out at Imperial—down south of Ogallala—breaking into places and stealing what they wanted. That was in 1961, in the wintertime, with snow on the ground. Well, they came into town here one night and broke into Ewoldt's store. Ewoldt lives upstairs, but they didn't know that, and he heard them messing around and called me at home, and I came driving up and caught them up by the depot. They were in their sock feet, trying on a bunch of cowboy boots they'd stole. Their car was full of fancy shirts and Stetson hats and forty-dollar boots—all kinds of cowboy stuff. I got them out of their car and had the driver standing with his hands on the roof in the regular way, and I was frisking him. Well, all of a sudden the other boy came around the car, and when I looked up he had a revolver in his hand. I slipped behind the driver. My gun was an old .351 automatic—what they call a riot gun. I told the boy to drop that revolver. But the driver gave a jump and pushed up my gun, and before I could get it back in position the other boy fired his revolver. I don't know how he missed me, but he did. He hit the driver instead—hit him in the arm. My gun was ready then, and I fired and hit him at the belt, on the buckle, and staggered him against the car. I told him to drop his gun. But he didn't. He up and shot me. Shot me in the left side, and the bullet went through both lobes of my liver. All I felt was like a hot poker or something touching me there. But I dropped my gun and sat down in a snowdrift. The boys jumped back in their car and made to drive off. But before they more than got started I reached around and found my gun and fired and shot out their front tire. The driver jumped out yelling and put his hand up—his good hand. But the other one, he was still acting up. He called me a dirty s.o.b. and a lot worse, and started shooting at me again. So I did the same. He was leaning over the top of the car, and my first shot only hit the shoulder padding on his coat. Then I shot into the car and blew out the windows in his face. He couldn't see with all that glass flying, but I didn't feel like shooting anymore, and Don Vetter came running up, and that was it. They hauled the three of us off to the hospital at North Platte to get patched up. I was laid up there for quite a few weeks. One of the boys turned out to be fourteen years old, and the other one was fifteen. They both got something like eighteen months of correction. The boy that did all the shooting, he came out and turned into a pretty solid citizen. I understand he's never given anybody any more trouble. But the other boy—I don't know. I never heard."

The principal business of the courthouse is the farms and ranches of Logan County. Their needs and responsibilities make up most of the routine work of the county clerk and the county treasurer and the county judge and the county commissioners, and they are the entire concern of the county agent and the two Department of Agriculture agencies. The Logan county agent is also the county agent of McPherson County, the neighboring county on the west. This gives him a district almost the size of Delaware. He is a crewcut young man with a faraway look named Edmond A. Cook. "This is conservative country," he told me. "There are progressive people—people who adapt to the modern world—but the other kind are still around. 'Conservative' isn't really the right word. The people I mean are rigid. They're self-sufficient and individualistic. They still have the pioneer mentality. Their grandfathers *were* the pioneers out here. Well, a county agent is an educator. My job is to take the research information from the experimental stations and get it to the farmers in a form they can use. This means meetings and workshops, and the subjects are insect problems, crops—feed crops— and irrigation. We've got an interesting project going on now. It's a new way of growing corn in this dry country. Sod corn, we call it. There's no tillage—you plant rows of corn in the untouched sod. The growth of the grass is retarded chemically for about thirty days. That gives the corn a head start. Then the grass comes along in the normal way and holds the soil between the rows, and after the corn is harvested the grass is there for fall pasture and cover through the winter. The sod is precious here. The wind is the enemy. We have plenty of water, but it's all underground. There's an ocean of pure water, the sweetest in the world, under these Sand Hills. The trouble is we get only about eighteen inches of rain a year —about half of what you get back East—and the wind blows all the time. The sod is the only thing that keeps the land from blowing away. We almost lost it back in the thirties, you know. I don't know how our sod-corn project will work out. There are people who will give it serious attention. But there are those who won't. They're still back there with the homesteaders who wouldn't change—who kept on plowing the dust and overgrazing the range. Nobody can tell them anything. They have to be in pretty bad trouble before they'll come to me for help."

The U.S.D.A. agencies that have offices in the court-house are the Agricultural Stabilization and Conservation Service and the Soil Conservation Service. Each consists of a manager and a couple of women clerks. The Agricultural Stabilization and Conservation Service administers the federal crop-control (or production-adjustment) program, and it has been represented in Stapleton since 1959 by a native of Tryon (and a former rancher and Army officer) named William Griffith. "I'm a native and I'm prejudiced," he told me, "but I've observed a good many other places, and the Sand Hills country is hard to beat for good living. You can buy a half of beef that you've selected yourself, and Ewoldt's will butcher it and age it and keep it for you in their locker. Or a lamb or a hog. There's good pheasant shooting and good deer hunting— did you ever taste venison salami? The people are friendly —everybody knows everybody's business. We have very little changeover. People come here and they don't want to leave. Our teachers stay on forever. We have only one serious problem. It's the economic problem that's threatening all of rural and small-town America. We can't keep our young people. The farms and ranches are getting bigger and bigger and more and more mechanized, and the jobs are getting fewer and fewer. Not many of our local boys can hope to make a living here. They want to stay, but they can't—not unless they make a special effort. My youngest son is at the University of Nebraska, and his plan is to be a veterinarian so he can stay on here in the Sand Hills. Randy Joe Kramer, the salutatorian of the senior class at the high school this year, is another example. He's going to the university to study agriculture. He wants to be a county agent. On the other hand, there are John Beckius's two sons. They're more typical. There wasn't anything for them here. One of them is working down at the Platte, and the other is out in Denver."

The manager of the Soil Conservation Service office is a broad, smiling, bespectacled man (with brown eyes) named John H. Sautter. Sautter is a former high-school teacher and an authority on the pasture grasses of western Nebraska, and his job is counseling the ranchers of Logan and McPherson counties on how to preserve and improve their range. The experience has given him a view of human nature much like that of the county agent, Cook. "The better the rancher, the more apt he is to ask us for help," he told me. "The poor ones don't bother. It's like everything else—the less you know, the less you want to know." I spent an afternoon out in the field with Sautter. He had been asked by a prosperous rancher to draft an improvement program for some grassland a few miles north of town, and we drove out there together in a government pickup truck that was geared to riding the range.

It was a beautiful afternoon, with a high, blue sky and a horizon of great white clouds and a cooling flow of breeze. There was a meadowlark on almost every fence post, and a ring of old automobile tires laid flat around the foot of every telephone pole. The meadowlark is the state bird of Nebraska, and it has the distinction, now rare among state birds (how often does one see a bluebird in New York?), of being ubiquitous in its state. The tires are a protective contrivance peculiar to the Sand Hills. "Cattle are one of the problems of a cattle range," Sautter told me. "Cattle like to scratch themselves, and they particularly like to scratch against a pole where they can circle around and around. Those tires keep them back and away. They don't like the feel of them underfoot. Otherwise, they'd go scratching around until they dug a trench in the ground and the pole got loose and fell out. Their trails are almost as bad. Cattle are great creatures of habit. They'll follow the same little track through a gap in the hills until they've dug a trench, and with the kind of wind we have out here it doesn't take long for a trench to grow into a gully."

We turned off the highway at an opening in the fence and went over a gridiron cattle guard. We headed across a range hub-deep in grass. There were cattle grazing on a slope in the distance, and off to the right was the long green wall of a windbreak. "This country was practically treeless in the Indian-and-buffalo days," Sautter told me. "The only trees were along the Platte and the Dismal River, up north, and some of the little creeks. The windbreaks are all man-made. The early settlers planted them with trees they hauled all the way up from the river bottoms. That's why you see so many cottonwoods. A cottonwood will grow from a slip, like a willow. Windbreaks are part of my job. A lot of the big ones around here were put in back in the thirties. Some of them are a mile long. Shelter belts, they called them then. Those were desperate years. People had the idea that trees would increase the humidity. It was a survival of the kind of wishful thinking that told the first settlers that rain followed the plow. In the thirties, they thought trees would bring rain. They thought they would break the drought. The design of a windbreak depends on the site, and also on what it's specifically for—to shelter your house or your livestock, or to protect a field or an orchard or a garden. We think a windbreak should be at least four rows deep. Five is better. The conventional design puts tall, broadleaf trees, like ash or Chinese elm, in the middle and smaller, denser evergreens, like pines and cedars, in the outer rows. My own preference is for exclusively pine and cedar. That windbreak over there is one of the older ones. It's a mixture of various plantings—box elder, Chinese elm, Russian olive, cottonwood, cedar, and even some wild plum. And if you'll look up there—off near the end—do you see something moving? That's a little herd of antelope."

We bumped slowly on across the range. The range was not entirely grass. There were occasional scatterings of wild flowers—blue pentstemon, yellow wild mustard, orange gromwell. We cut around the side of a hill and labored up an easier slope and came out on a windy plateau. The range spread out below us. A tiny car crept along the faraway highway. Sautter stopped the truck and rolled down his window. "This is excellent range," he said. "It's in good condition, too. Predominantly sand bluestem. That little shrublike plant you see here and there is a legume we call leadplant. When you see it growing undisturbed like that, it's an indication of good range condition. It means the cattle have plenty of other things to eat. They'll eat leadplant, but generally not until they've grazed off the best of the grass. It's a different story down there in the valley. This is natural range up here. The valley has been farmed, and the native grasses are just about gone. What you see there is panic grass and six-week fescue and western ragweed. And a little buffalo grass. You probably can't see the buffalo grass. It's real short—never gets higher than four or five inches. I happen to know it's there. People are always talking and writing about buffalo grass. I guess it sounds romantic. Buffalo grass is a native grass, but that doesn't make it desirable. It probably came in wherever the buffalo overgrazed the range. It has one good use. It's tough and will stand a lot of traffic. We use it around here in the outfield in the ballparks. It's going to take work to bring that valley back. The homesteaders did just about everything they could to ruin this land. They never learned to understand it. They grew a lot of corn because corn was what they knew. That bared the soil at planting time in the spring, and then in the fall they turned the cows into the corn to graze. That kept the land open all through the winter. Corn exhausts the soil, and open soil blows. The only reason most of those people quit farming here was they had nothing left to farm. The people now know better—most of them, anyway. This is grazing land. And when it's maintained right, it's about the best there is."

Sautter rolled up his window and sat back in his seat. "The only thing we can't control is fire," he said. "Prairie fires are a constant threat, and they're almost always acts of God. Nobody in this country is crazy enough to drop a cigarette on the range. The usual cause of a prairie fire is lightning. Practically all the fires that the Stapleton fire department goes out on are prairie fires. And they can be bad—real bad. I don't know if you've noticed my hands and my neck and chin. That's all grafted skin. I got involved in a prairie fire a few years back—in March of 1967. It was a windy day, and dry like it usually is, and the grass was about a foot high. I was driving out of town, and I saw some smoke in the hills out south. When a man sees a fire around here, he generally tries to do something about it. We all of us carry a shovel in our cars. Well, I headed that way, and there was a ranch house nearby and I stopped and asked if they had called the fire department, and the woman said she had. But I thought I could do a little something in the meantime. So I went on to the fire. I left my pickup truck on the road and got out my shovel and went through the fence to the range. The fire was burning northwest to southeast. I went down the west side of the fire line, digging and throwing dirt. I worked for about a quarter of a mile. I had it out except for a few stems and chips, and I started back to the pickup. It was then that the wind took a change. It swung around to blowing from the northeast, and it picked up to about sixty miles an hour, and a few smolderings blew into some fresh grass. It went up like a bomb. I was about forty feet from the new line, and it had me cut off from the pickup—it was a couple of hundred yards away. I saw that big wall of fire coming at me, and I knew I was up the creek. You can't get away from a grass fire. You can't outrun it. All you can do is hope for the best and go through it. People have done it and come out the other side. The trouble is a fire like that burns up all the oxygen in the air. It's hard to get a good breath, and I was half worn out from shoveling. Anyway, I ran, but I lost control and I tripped and fell and went down. I lay there—I couldn't move—and the fire burned over, under, and around me. I had on an insulated coat and boots and cap. But my pants, they were permanent-press synthetic—the kind that gets hot and stays hot. And my gloves were in my pocket. So my hands and my legs and part of my face got cooked. I don't know how long I lay there. I got to my feet somehow and got myself back to the pickup—the fire had left me far behind—and got it started and drove till I met the fire trucks coming out from town. The funny thing is it was only then that I started to hurt. They got me into the ambulance and we started for North Platte. Then I really began to hurt. I couldn't wait to get to the hospital, and I thought I'd never leave it. They had me there for three full months, and I hurt every minute of that time until the last two days."

There are one hundred and fifty-five agricultural holdings in Logan County. One hundred and sixteen of them are classified as farms, and thirty-nine are ranches. Most of the farmers run a few cattle, but their principal crop is grain—feed grain and a little wheat. The farms range in size from around a section (six hundred and forty acres) to about two thousand acres, and (for reasons of soil quality and availability of water) they are confined to a narrow belt along the southern edge of the county. The rest of the county is cattle country. There are a few ranches in Logan County of around three thousand acres, but most of them are larger. Small ranches are impractical in the Sand Hills; it takes about twenty acres of such range to support a cow and her calf. Most of the Logan County ranches are profitable enterprises. In 1969, they marketed a total of fifteen thousand five hundred calves, at an average price of a hundred and twenty dollars a head, and received a gross return of just under two million dollars. The biggest ranch in Logan County is owned by Peter Kiewit & Sons (the family concern that also owns the Omaha *World-Herald*) and totals around thirty thousand acres. The Milldale Ranch Company (whose brand—a sort of gothic H—is the oldest registered brand in Nebraska) embraces twenty-nine thousand acres, and other important operations include the Logan County Land & Cattle Co. ranch (twenty-three thousand acres), the Baskin Diamond-Bar Ranch (fourteen thousand acres), the Santo Land & Cattle Co. (ten thousand acres), and the Wayne Salisbury ranch, with seven thousand acres of uncommonly good range.

The Baskin ranch is the biggest ranch in the neighborhood of Stapleton still owned by the founding family. Its present proprietor is a tall, leathery man of seventy-two named Robert Baskin. The ranch house is just outside town, a bit north of the railroad tracks and the depot. I walked out and called on Baskin there one Saturday afternoon. He led me across a dining room furnished with a Duncan Phyfe table and cabinets full of Haviland china, and into an office hung with family photographs. He put me in a comfortable chair and sat down at a rolltop desk. "Life has treated me all right," he told me. "My dad founded this ranch and got it going, and I've got me a real good son-in-law to carry it on. I mean Dave Jones. Dave more or less runs the Diamond-Bar now, and it couldn't be in better hands. My dad used to say he was

planting trees for me. I planted them for my daughter, and now Dave is planting them for their children. I like to think the Diamond-Bar will last. Our brand is an old brand. It's up there close to the Milldale H. My dad bought it off a couple of bachelor brothers from Denmark who homesteaded here in the very early years. He got the money to start this ranch by cutting meat in North Platte and buying and selling Indian horses in the summer. He started out with twelve hundred acres, and he added to it bit by bit—a section or two at a time. I brought it up to its present size. All the ranches around here are made up of bits and pieces. Nobody's ranch is just right. There are always gaps, so you have to cross your neighbor when you move your cattle. I have some good neighbors and I have some not so good. I can get along with anybody who treats me halfway right. But I sure don't believe in being pushed over and walked the full length of. Western hospitality is practically a thing of the past. One of my neighbors had a branding. I went over to help out, and I brought along a couple of my men. Then, a week or so later, I'm branding, and my neighbor comes over to help. But he only brings *one* hand. That isn't what I call hospitality. Wayne Salisbury is branding today, and Dave and two of our hands are over there helping out. Wayne isn't the neighbor I was talking about. We're branding here next Saturday, and I know Wayne will be here with two of his men to help. Nobody can brand without his neighbors in to help. We sell around nine hundred calves a year, and we'll be branding about six hundred of them next week. Everybody wants to expand his operation. Raising cattle is the world's biggest gambling den, and you can't win unless you've got some size. When I was buying a lot of land, back in the middle thirties, you could get it for two or three dollars an acre. Now it's sky-high. It's sixty, seventy, even eighty dollars an acre. The way prices are today, a man can't make a living ranching unless he's already got his ranch. It's impossible to start from scratch. It would mean a capital outlay of almost a quarter of a million dollars for even a little ranch—for only three thousand acres. A man couldn't live long enough to get his money back on an investment like that. And that's just for land. We're all of us mechanized now. We don't need but six or eight hands to run the Diamond-Bar in summer, and in winter there's just two hands and Dave and me. We used to have one man did nothing but ride the range and check up on fences and if the windmills and water tanks were working all right. Some people ride the range in a truck these days, or on a motorbike. We do it by plane. Dave has a little Cessna Skylark. He can check on forty windmills in thirty minutes. I don't mean to say that we've given up the horse. You can't haul a bull out of a spring hole with a motorcycle. And you can't brand and notch and inoculate and castrate without some horses and riders to rope your calves. We have about a hundred head of horses. They're mostly quarterhorses. We break and sell a lot of them to stables and such back East. To towns and cities everywhere. There's nothing new about country people leaving the farm and moving into town. But now it looks like the horse is following them in."

Baskin drove me back to the Motel in an air-conditioned Cadillac. He raised a hand in greeting to everybody on the street, and everybody waved to him. He let me off in front of the Cafe. Several boys were lounging there, and I knew two of them. They were the Perry boys —Robert, a senior at the high school, and his fifteen-year-old brother, Monty Joe. Monty had a bandage around his forehead.

"What happened to you?" I said.

Robert laughed. "He got himself kicked by a calf," he said.

"I sure did," Monty said. "I sure guess I did. It was out at the Salisbury branding this morning. One of the riders dragged up a calf, and me and the guy I was working with grabbed him to hold for the brand and the other stuff they do. But he was laying the wrong way. The Salisbury brand goes on the left side. So we made to flip him over and I was holding his front legs and one of them broke loose and kicked me. Those calves are only a couple of months old, but they're strong, and when they smell that hot iron coming at them it's like they get stronger. We had a calf one time that strained so hard he actually ruptured himself. And I guess those little hoofs are sharp. One of the cowboys drove me in to the Platte, and the doctor had to take nine stitches. But you know what? On the way in, we were going about ninety miles an hour, and the Highway Patrol stopped us. But when they saw what the trouble was, they waved us right on. They let us get up to almost a hundred."

The pastor of St. John's Church is a young Nebraskan named John Schlaf. Stapleton is his first parish. "I spent last week where I could see nothing but dead concrete and the hurrying footsteps of man," Father Schlaf told me. "I was at a conference in Omaha. When I got home last night, I felt the difference. I felt the expanse, the space, some reflection of God in the countryside. Down there, I felt closed in—uptight. Down in Missouri, when I was in seminary, I used to think of working in Los Angeles. They need priests there. But then I got more realistic and saw that I was rurally oriented. I grew up a little east of here, in the little town of Spalding. And Omaha isn't even a city in big-city terms. But, of course, I'm a natural celibate. I like privacy. I don't even have a housekeeper here. If I'd wanted a housekeeper, I'd have got married. Stapleton is an ideal kind of parish for a priest like me—a little break for rest and study. I'll be moving on. But I could stay here for the rest of my life and love every month of it. It's a real parish, everybody participates, it's a community, it's beautiful. Everybody knows if somebody needs help, and they see that he gets it. We have some poor people here. They're poor by national income standards. But they don't know it—their needs are small. And if you called them poor, they'd be indignant. They'd be insulted. Stapleton is still remote.

The war and the riots and the drugs and the pollution—they seem so far away. And race. Mexicans can't belong to the Elks down in North Platte. That bugs a lot of us, but that's the only race problem here. They've got some Jewish people in North Platte, but I never heard a word of anti-Semitism. Everybody here is sympathetic to civil rights. Of course, it's well removed. There aren't any Negroes in western Nebraska. But if a few Negro families moved into town, our people would lean over backward to be friendly. But if more than a few moved in—I don't know. They'd probably begin to feel threatened. I'm sure of one thing. These are good, Christian people, peace-loving people, but if a hippie group showed up here looking for wild marijuana and everything else, I'd be worried. There'd be bloodshed. These people would stomp on them."

My last day in Stapleton was a Saturday. That night, after supper, after packing my bags, after a farewell walk around town (up to the depot and down to the school), I dropped into the Wagon Wheel Tavern for a farewell glass of beer. There was only a handful of people there. I saw James Morey playing the pinball machine, Wayne Salisbury with a group at the bar, Grace Young at a table with her father drinking a Coke and eating a bowl of popcorn. Elwin Miller and his wife, a pretty, red-haired girl, were sitting in a booth, and they called to me to join them. We sat and talked and drank Hamm's beer and listened to two cowboys with crewcuts and long sideburns arguing about Clint Eastwood (his age and origins and whether he could actually ride a horse or if he used a double) until about eleven o'clock. The Millers drove off to a dance at Mullen, some sixty miles away, and I walked back to the Motel. Except for the cars nosed in at the Wagon Wheel, the street was empty, and the only light was the wild green mercury glare of the street light at the Corner and a glow behind the barred back window of the post office. The only sound was the wind—the hot, dry, everlasting wind—stirring the cottonwood trees.

Forty Flights of Steps

Driving west around the end of April through southern West Virginia, I stopped for the night at the mountain town of Welch. I stopped there for a night, and I stayed on for almost a week. Welch (pop. 4,149) is the seat of McDowell County, and McDowell County is Appalachia—the quintessence of Appalachia. It is rich in coal and poor in people. It is the home of a metallurgical coal favorably known throughout the industrial world as Pocahontas No. 3, and the birthplace of the federal food-stamp program. Its mines have never been more productive (or its working miners better paid), but since the mid-nineteen-fifties, when the continuous loader and other automated apparatuses were first introduced, the number of men employed in the McDowell County mines has fallen from twenty thousand to seven thousand. The population of the county has also sharply declined. It dropped from 98,887 in 1950 to 71,359 in 1960, and then to 50,400 in 1970, and many towns that were flourishing at the time of the Second World War are all but ghost towns now. I learned these facts in the course of my stay in Welch. They were not, however, what kept me there. I stayed because of the mountains.

McDowell County is as mountainous as my Long Island home is flat. It covers an area of five hundred and thirty-three square miles, and almost all of it is mountains—big, crowded, convoluted mountains. There is no ruggeder country anywhere east of the Rockies. The mountains are steep, with many cliffs and outcrop ledges, and the slopes are thickly grown with hickory and hemlock and oak and maple and groves of giant rhododendron. They rise—eight hundred, a thousand, fifteen hundred feet—to razorback ridges, and the valleys between are little more than ravines. Most of the valleys are river valleys, and most of the rivers are rushing mountain streams. The Tug Fork River, the biggest of these, has an average fall of ten feet to the mile. There is very little level land in the county (only two per cent of the total area has a slope of less than twelve feet in a hundred), and all of it is in the river valleys. So are all the towns. They are long, narrow towns—a mountainside and river, a street of stores and houses, a railroad track, and another rising mountain. Welch is a maze of narrow streets and old brick buildings. It lies in a pocket of bottomland at the confluence of Elkhorn Creek, Brown's Creek, and the Tug Fork, and it is walled around with mountains.

I stayed in Welch at the Carter Hotel. Five stories high, built of orange brick and white marble, a comfortable relic of the coal boom of the twenties, the Carter occupies a corner at the intersection of McDowell Street, which runs north-south, and a steep, dead-end street called Bank Street. McDowell is one-way, just wide enough for two cars to move abreast, and flanked by four-foot sidewalks, but it is the main street of Welch. It follows the course of the Tug Fork River for most of its way through town. Across the river there is only a railroad track—a branch line of the Norfolk & Western. My room at the Carter was a corner room on the second floor, and it looked south along McDowell. Standing there on my first morning in town, I could see the U.S. Jewelers, the Flat Iron Drug Store, Bobo's Barbershop. Then came the mouth of an alley. Then the flank of a three-level parking garage. Then a five-story red brick building. Then the side of a wooded mountain. That was all. There was no sky. The mountain closed the view.

Every view in Welch is closed by a mountain. "Some of these mountains have names," Hobart Payne, the municipal recorder, told me in his office in City Hall. "They got around to naming some, and some they didn't bother. I guess we've got too many." City Hall fronts on Elkhorn Street, and Elkhorn Street fronts on Elkhorn Creek, and across the creek is the rise of another mountain. "That mountain you're looking at, they call it Mitchell Mountain," Payne said. "Those buildings off to the right up there on the slope are the high school and the junior high. The mountain looks real pretty now, with the trees in leaf and the sun shining down and all. But you ought to see it in the winter. It makes the day pretty short. When I see the sun on those steps leading up to the school, I know it's almost time for lunch. The winter sun don't come over the top of Mitchell Mountain until just about half past ten. And, of course, we don't have it very long. The sun sets here on a winter day about half past two in the afternoon. As a matter of fact, the days aren't any too long here in Welch at any time of year. Sunrise this morning was five-fifteen, according to the almanac, but, if you happened to notice, it wasn't real light until almost seven-thirty."

Welch High School stands far above town but far below the summit of Mitchell Mountain. The steps leading up to it begin at a footbridge on Elkhorn Street, which crosses Elkhorn Creek just opposite City Hall. It is a climb of fourteen steps from the end of the bridge to a narrow, hillside cross street of tall, hillside houses. This is Virginia Avenue. Ten more steps and a sidewalk ramp lead to a flight of forty-three steps, and these lead up to Maple Avenue, another cross street cut into the face of the mountain. A double stairway of sixteen steps circles up and around a terrace to the door of the school, which looks steeply down on Maple Avenue. "We've got four full stories here," William Belcher, the custodian, told me. "Five, counting the basement, where I've got my office. But I operate all over the building, and it's ninety-six steps from here on up to the top. Ninety-six steps, and I'm up there a dozen, fourteen times a day. I'll tell you something else. I grew up running the ridges. I was born out east of town, on Belcher Mountain. But I never knew what climbing was until I took this job. It don't seem to bother the kids. I guess the exercise is good for them. By the same token, this ought to be a healthy town. Everybody gets their exercise here. They can't very well avoid it. You can't walk anywhere in Welch without climbing up or down a hill. And you almost have to walk. I mean, you can't drive your car. Oh, you can drive it, but you can't find a place to park. Most of our streets aren't wide enough for parking. That's residential and business streets both. Some of them aren't even wide enough for side-walks, and plenty have only one. The few streets here that are wide enough for parking, they're all set up with parking meters. So any place you find to park, it's going to cost you money. The only free parking in town is your own garage, if you've got one. Some people don't. They don't have the space. This town has its faults. These mountains are a problem. But it's like a fellow I had here one time used to say—how many places do you know where you can stand at the basement door and spit on the roof of a three-story house?"

Parking is a municipal monopoly in Welch. Only the town has had the ways and means to produce the necessary space. A plaque on the big parking garage on Mc-Dowell Street proclaims it to be "The First Municipally Owned Parking Building in the United States. Dedicated September, 1941." Two parking lots—one a little beyond the McDowell Street garage and the other across town—are also products of municipal ingenuity. Part of the McDowell Street lot is a shelf across the mouth of Elkhorn Creek. The other lot consists entirely of a platform spanning the Elkhorn for a distance of three hundred and twenty feet (with space for sixty cars), and it is engineered in such a way that water can flow harmlessly across it in time of flood. There are, in addition, a second parking garage (on Bank Street), a third parking lot, and several hundred metered parking spaces. The rates are low—paternalistically low (ten cents for an hour in a metered space, and off-street parking is even cheaper)—but the municipal parking system nevertheless produces

an annual revenue of about a hundred and twenty thousand dollars. "We don't have a whole lot of crime in Welch," B. E. Dodson, the chief of police, told me. "Oh, we get a little breaking and entering, and sometimes a drifter comes through and maybe tries to steal a car. That's about the extent of it. I hope it stays that way. I mean, it better. I don't know how we'd manage otherwise. The police department operates the parking system, and that's practically a full-time job. That's why I've got my office here in the main garage. I've only got but twelve men, including my assistant, and we do it all—twenty-four hours a day. And the traffic. We got no time to spare for crime. The traffic here—well, I've been to some real cities, and I've seen some traffic problems. But you take a Friday afternoon right here, with the town full of folks looking to spend their paychecks and their food stamps and their unemployment and their social security and their black lung and their everything else—I call that traffic. And speeding. You wouldn't think it was possible to speed on the kind of streets we have in Welch, but they do. The kids do. They even some of them drag. You know Matney's junkyard, out south of town? They won't even take your car anymore. They got enough."

There are six automobile agencies in Welch. They serve the town and most of McDowell County. The largest agency (with two showrooms) is Hall Chevrolet-Oldsmobile, Inc. "We also handle Jeeps," John R. Hall, the president, told me. "This is good country for Jeeps. It's good country for any kind of car. I can sell all the Oldses I can get. These people are crazy about cars. We sell around three hundred and fifty new and seven hundred and fifty used cars a year. We sold a hundred and ten last month alone. And the other dealers—they aren't hurting, either. People really love cars here. Go up a hollow and look at the houses. They're pretty sorry, most of them. But look at the cars out front. Count them. If there's five in the family over sixteen years of age, they've got five cars. A car is something they can spend their money on. It's something to do. They like to drive. They like to drive it hard. They don't care that the roads are narrow and winding and full of holes. You can hit a hole *this* deep on any highway in the county. But they don't care. They don't let that bother them. These people can total a car like nobody else in the world. We've got two tow trucks here and we can't begin to keep up with the wrecks. Look at that red Camaro out there in back. Look at that front end. I don't know if it's even worth repairing. And, shoot, it isn't more than four months old."

Accidents are a commonplace on the hillside streets and switchback roads of Welch and the surrounding county. I read about them every day in the Welch *Daily News* ("Two Injured in Highway Wreck"), and the signs are everywhere—a streak of sudden tire skids, a broken guardrail cable, a totaled car at the bottom of a ravine. One afternoon on Warren Street—a riverside street so narrow that I had to back up half a block to let an approaching car get past me—I counted the splattered corpses of a dog, a cat, two squirrels, and a rabbit. "You

can always tell an out-of-stater by the way he handles his car," a state trooper assigned to McDowell County told me. "He creeps. He brakes. He's scared to death of those drops. Some visitors park their car and won't touch it again until it's time to leave. The natives understand the roads. They think they do, anyway. Still, we average maybe thirty accidents a month around the county that are serious enough to call the police. The funny thing is they're very few of them collisions. Most of our accidents, and practically all our fatalities, involve just one vehicle." There was a report of such an accident in the *Daily News* on my second day in Welch. It read:

Tony Joe (Tommy) Craig, 40, of Welch, miraculously escaped death or serious injury early this morning when a car he was driving plunged several hundred feet off Hobart Street and down a hillside, lodging between a stone wall and the Joe Rucci home on lower McDowell Street, Welch Police Lt. Adolph Bary reported.

The vehicle was demolished, and local police and members of the fire department worked for almost an hour before freeing Craig from the twisted wreckage. He was rushed to Stevens Clinic, where he was under observation for a neck injury. He is also reported to have suffered some cuts and bruises.

Bary said he and Patrolman Estil Halsey are continuing an investigation in an effort to learn the cause of the accident. The 1954 Chevrolet bounced off a high rock cliff and then rolled down the hillside. The incident occurred about 3:30 A.M., while Craig was enroute home from downtown Welch, Bary said.

I read the report as it came from the press at the offices of the *Daily News*. "I'd call that a little unusual," C. H. Hardison, the managing editor, told me. "They don't usually survive. But we get a lot of those over-the-cliff accidents. We've got a lot of cliffs. I had an accident like that happen at my house a few years ago. It was early in the morning, in the winter, in February. I live out south, on Summers Street, down by the river, and a woman came along on the street above and hit some ice on a curve and went through the wire fence they have there and came down my backyard hill and knocked down an apple tree I'd finally got to grow there and slammed into the back of my house. She hit the house at the second floor and then came sliding down, and she took the bathroom window and a whole wall of aluminum siding with her. I called the fire department and the police, and they came, and all they said was, 'Get a blanket.'"

I walked up to Hobart Street for a look at the scene of Tony Joe Craig's miraculous escape. To get there, I climbed a street (Court Street) so steep that the sidewalk began and ended as a flight of steps. There are houses—most of them four-story houses—standing shoulder to shoulder on the upper side of Hobart Street on terraced lots secured by a twelve-foot stone retaining wall, and the front doors are reached by flights of twenty and thirty, and even forty, steps. A few of the houses (six in a block of twenty) have garages—little caves dug into the mountain and framed by the retaining wall. Hobart Street is eighteen feet wide, and there is a three-foot sidewalk along the upper side. The other side of the street is a drop of at least three hundred feet to a thrust of rooftops below. I expected to locate the scene by finding a gap in a fence or guardrail. But there is no fence or guardrail the length of Hobart Street. There is only a curbing about four inches high. I never found where the car went over. It could have jumped the curbing at almost any point from one end of the street to the other.

The mayor of Welch is a tall, thin Republican (in a Democratic town) named William B. Swope, and he is also its leading real-estate broker. His real-estate business occupies the ground floor of a three-story brick building on McDowell Street. The upper floors are divided into apartments. "You won't find many buildings here in Welch that don't have a couple of floors of apartments up above," he told me. "People have to have someplace to live. I've done all right in the real-estate business, but real estate is a problem here. We've got a lot of mountains, but we don't have any land, and what we have is rarely on the market. The first thing you want to understand is that most of the land in McDowell County—well, a good third of it, anyway—is owned by just one company. I mean the Pocahontas Land Corporation, and the Pocahontas Land Corporation is a subsidiary of the Norfolk & Western Railway Company. They don't do any mining. They lease the rights to the coal companies and to people like U.S. Steel. They're ready to lease, but they hate to sell. The other big owners—Berwind Land Corporation and Consolidation Coal Company—they think pretty much the same. They will almost never sell you any land in fee. The most you can buy is just the surface. They retain the mineral rights. They're not going to let you have what might be a rich seam of coal. That's only sensible. And the reason they don't like to sell even the surface is this. This country is riddled with coal mines. There are miles of mines right under the city of Welch. And they're always opening new ones. Well, suppose you built a house and the land underneath gave way and the house fell into the mine. They don't want to worry about lawsuits. But the result is a hell of a problem. We don't even own a city dump. We rent five acres in a hollow out west of town. The only sewage-treatment plant in the county is one that U.S. Steel built out at Gary, five miles south of here. I've got plans for one here in Welch. I've got my eye on a site at the north end of town where we could build an oxidation ditch. Our sewage now goes into the river. I was able to put in a pipe that carries it downstream, out of town. But we'll solve those problems. We've got a good hundred years of coal still left to mine. The big problem is housing. You've seen the houses here in town. There's no such thing as level land, and if you've got a lot as big as seventy-five by a hundred feet you've practically got an estate. I know houses that aren't fit for a hog. Dirty. Fallen down. Hung on the side of a mountain halfway up some hollow. But people will jump at the chance to buy them and fix them up. We've got a hospital here that's offering a guarantee of fifty thousand a year for a doctor. They can't get one. They drive into town with their wives, and she won't even get out of the car. The hills and the roads and no place to build a nice big house—it scares them all away. But goddamn it. They don't realize. This place could be another Switzerland."

Mayor Swope himself is comfortably housed. He lives in a nice big stone house with a double gallery across the front, and it stands on a shelf of terraced lawn high up on Mitchell Mountain. I saw it in his company a day or two after our meeting. We approached it along a climbing, winding private road that ended at the door of a garage cut into the mountain slope. The house was directly below the garage, and below the house—far, far below—lay all of Welch. A flight of (thirty-four) stone steps led down to the house. "My grandfather built this house in 1903," Swope told me. "Welch was just beginning then, and there were a lot of highly skilled Indian stone-masons around. 'Tallies,' they called them. The retaining walls you see all over town, the Tallies built them all. Beautiful work. But a lost art now. Now it's all poured concrete, and it ain't worth a damn. It won't last—it doesn't have the weight, it doesn't have the strength. The Tallies built this house. They dug the stone out of the hillside here. They shot and chipped and did it all by hand. It's still as sound as solid rock. I haven't had to do hardly a thing. I *did* put in our road. In my grandfather's time and in my father's time and until not too many years ago, the only way to get to this house was from the street

below. That's Maple Avenue way down there, and there are a hundred and sixty-three steps between the street and our front door. My wife and I and our two boys and a girl, we all walked up and down those steps every day of our lives, but we had a winch and a basket on a cable for packages and groceries and stuff. We heated the house with coal. Everything is natural gas here now. That's another thing I've done as mayor, and the city is a little cleaner. Nobody burns coal now except a few miners. They get it at reduced rates by contract. Pocahontas No. 3 is too expensive to burn for heat. Twenty dollars a ton. They only use it for coke. But in the old days you burned coal or nothing, and getting it up the mountain to this house was a problem. My grandfather solved it by having his own mine. A lot of people did the same. Our mine is back there under the garage. It runs back into the mountain for about a thousand feet, and we had a man to dig it for us. He pushed it out on a car on a little track. I walled our mine up ten years ago. We had a miner killed in there. I'll never open it again—not unless I need a bomb shelter."

Most of the best houses in Welch are old houses, and most of them are acquired by inheritance. Few of them ever appear on the open market. "I guess you could say we inherited our house," Rollo L. Taylor, the publisher of the *Daily News*, told me. "We wouldn't be here if we hadn't. We're not natives. My wife is from Alabama, and I was working on the paper in Spartanburg, down in South Carolina, when we heard that the *Daily News* was coming up for sale. That was in 1963, and we had a baby and we wanted a paper of our own. We came up here and looked the situation over, and everything looked all right —except for a place to live. You've seen some of the houses here. But we were lucky. The publisher of the paper wanted to move away, so we ended up buying his house along with the paper. It's a good brick house, well built and plenty of room (we've got two children now), and we even have a little lawn. A *level* lawn." Other couples new to Welch have had a less hospitable welcome. They have found that the acquisition of a house costs more than merely money. It also calls for patience, vigilance, and an elastic adaptability. "We moved here about ten years ago," Mrs. Edward Jarvis, Jr., told me. "My husband is an inspector-at-large for the State Department of Mines, and we were living up in Fayette County. Then he was transferred to this area. He came down first. He got a room in a motel and started looking around. It took him a month to find an apartment. It wasn't a real apartment. It was just four rooms on the top floor of a house on Court Street. So I came down and we moved in and I began looking for a real place to live—a house. I looked for eight years— eight solid *years*—and then a house turned up out in Junior Poca, out toward Gary. It was the very first house that became available in all those years, and we didn't hesitate. We took it. It's built on a fifteen-degree slope, and there's a long climb up to the front door, but we've got seven rooms, and it's wonderful to finally settle down."

There are about a dozen places to eat in Welch. Most of them are lunchrooms, diners, or drive-ins. I had most of my meals at a clean, well-lighted café (with a horseshoe counter, and tables with tablecloths, and booths around the walls) called the Mountaineer Restaurant. It occupies the ground floor of a two-story building on a corner of McDowell Street, just down the block from the Carter Hotel, and it is owned and operated by a Welchian of Italian descent named Quinto Bary. One morning, on my way to breakfast there, I happened to look up, and saw that the building was *not* a two-story building. It was a one-story building with a one-story house—a bungalow with a low-pitched roof—on top. The building was red brick, and the house was clapboard, painted red.

I had my breakfast and then looked around and found Bary sitting alone in a booth with a cup of coffee. "Oh, that," he told me. "That was all my wife. She got the brainstorm. We had a house—a regular house—but it wasn't what we wanted. But you can't buy a lot to build on in this town. Even if there was one, it would cost too much. We had this building, though, and my wife got to thinking. It was a good sound building, and the size was big enough—thirty-four by seventy-five feet. I went to a builder and talked about the cost of building something on the roof. The price he gave me, I decided to take a long gamble and build it myself, and I got a real good carpenter that was also willing to try. Weight was one problem, of course. And then there was how to get the material up there on the roof. For that, we built a ramp, like a switchback road, in the back. And to keep down the weight we used aluminum siding. That isn't clapboard, it's all aluminum. We worked out a lot of tricks for convenience. The windows are aluminum, and they lift out for washing. We couldn't stand the weight of a furnace, and the restaurant furnace here wouldn't handle the load, so we heat the house with electricity. We've got three bedrooms, two bathrooms, a big living room, a kitchen, a utility room, and plenty of closets. We've even got a terrace, like a roof garden, in the back. The only thing we haven't got that I'd like to have is a fireplace—too heavy. And the only trouble is that there's too much shade and it's hard to get anything to grow real good up there on the terrace."

There are no farms in McDowell County, and no commercial orchards. A few countrymen keep bees. Driving the mountain roads, I would sometimes see on a slope of a hollow a cluster of white box hives and mistake them for a moment for a row of headstones in a family burying ground. (There *are* a number of family burying grounds in McDowell County, but only two cemeteries. No room. One of the two, a hillside acre near Gary—half Protestant, half Catholic—has long since reached capacity. The only operating cemetery in the county is Iaeger Memorial Cemetery, on a long, climbing point of land at a bend in the Tug Fork River, just below a hamlet called Roderfield.) Even flower or vegetable gardens are rare. They are almost unheard of in town—in Welch. Few householders have space enough in the sun for more than a border of roses or a terraced row of tomatoes. Edward

Jarvis, the mine inspector, is one of these. "I've got the room," he told me. "And the slope isn't too bad. I've had pretty good luck with tomatoes and green beans and peppers and lettuce and even watermelon. The only trouble is the mountains. I've got an eastern exposure, and my garden gets the sun for only about three hours—from around eleven o'clock in the morning until two in the afternoon."

One of the biggest holders of tillable land in McDowell County is a wholesale-grocery salesman named Harry Wells. Wells lives a few miles south of Welch, on the road to Gary, and he has around five acres of level bottomland on the east bank of the Tug Fork River. "Let's stop here in the shade," he said to me. "This old cherry tree is a lifesaver on a hot day. And we get some hot days. It's nice and open in this part of the valley, so we're blessed with plenty of sun. Some of these hollows, they're no better than caves. Well, there's my land. It runs on down around that bend, and it's all good loam. No clay. No rocks. No coal. It's been tended for a good long time. I'm sixty-three years old, and my daddy was tending it before I was born. My daddy was a farmer—one of the last in the county. He used to grow corn on that hillside up there across the road. You look like you're wondering how. Well, those days are gone forever. You can't plow land that steep with a tractor. My daddy plowed with a mule. I've never really farmed myself, but I used to tend this bottom. But then I got a better idea. You know how folks live in Welch. They haven't got enough room to hardly even stretch, but a lot of them have that natural urge to plant a garden and see things grow. So I started renting out this land in little patches. I charge them ten dollars for a big enough strip, and I supply the water. I guess I could rent out twice as much land as I've got. Half of Welch does their gardening here. You know Rollo and Annis Taylor? Well, they've been growing stuff here for years. On a summer weekend, this place of mine is full of folks all down on their knees enjoying themselves. Some of them, they'll try anything. Mustard greens. Kale. Broccoli. Okra. Why, there's even some of them growing herbs."

I saw one other garden during my stay in McDowell County. This garden is also out toward Gary, and it is cultivated by a man named H. V. Ashley. Ashley owns and operates a big yellow clapboard railroad boarding house in a Norfolk & Western switchyard on the west bank of the Tug Fork. His place is bounded on the back and sides by acres of sidings and block-long strings of hopper-bottom coal cars, and on the front by the river. A swinging footbridge with a plank floor leads across the river to the road. (There are many such bridges in McDowell County. "I understand from my undertaker friends that there's nothing like a funeral where you have to carry the coffin across a swinging bridge," Rollo Taylor told me.) I had lunch one day at Ashley's place. The floor was grained and gritty with coal dust, and I ate on a stool at a counter—with a crowd of big, laughing, shouting, starving railroad men—to the rumble of locomotives and the clatter and shriek of hoppers. Lunch was pork chops, red beans, corn bread, and Dr. Pepper. After lunch, Ashley took me off in a four-wheel-drive pickup truck to see his garden. It was across the river, across the road, up a steep, sliding, coal-slag cart track, across a cascading brook on a railless bridge of railroad ties, and up a long hollow. We stopped near the head of the hollow at a garden plot about the size of a tennis court. Just beyond the garden were a little square brick building and a huge cylindrical pipe, like a silo laid on its side. The mouth of the pipe faced down the hollow, and it was fitted with a wire-mesh guard. Through the grille and down across the garden came a driving dynamo hum. "They call this Shaft Hollow," Ashley told me, "and that pipe there is the shaft. It's a ventilator shaft—the outflow from a U.S. Steel Company mine back under that mountain. The shaft is why I've got this garden here. The air blowing out of the mine is a constant sixty degrees, and that makes this end of the hollow like a greenhouse. We're up fairly high here—a couple of thousand feet—but I can put my garden in early. At least a month before the rest of them. And it produces long past frost. You wouldn't believe the crops I get. My sugar corn is six or seven feet high, compared with the average here of maybe four, and the first crop of beans I got last year was over a hundred bushels. I don't own this land, of course. It all belongs to Pocahontas, and they lease it out to U.S. Steel. But they don't care, either one of them, if I use it. They're only interested in coal. Listen how quiet it is up here. You don't hear nothing but that fan. This is what I call peaceful. It's soothing. Well, I'm going to drive you back a different way. It's around the side of the mountain, and you'll get a real nice view—right down on top of my place. My God, I remember one night. I was sitting at home and I heard a noise and I looked out and saw a light shining up on the road. I looked again, and it was a car laying on its back and with one of the head-lights shining. I ran out and up to the road and opened the door—and it was my best buddy laying dead across the wheel. He lived up this hollow and he knew the road, but I guess he did something wrong. I'll show you the place where he missed and went over."

On my way back to Welch, I picked up two hitchhiking teenage boys. They hailed me from an unpaved block of houses just north of Ashley's place, and I stopped and they climbed into the front seat beside me. They both wore bluejeans and striped sneakers, and one of them had a basketball under his arm. They weren't going in to town. Heck, no. They only wanted a lift down the road about a mile. They were local boys; their fathers both worked for U.S. Steel.

"My dad don't actually work in the mines," the boy with the basketball said. "He don't like it underground. He says it gives him that whatchamacallit phobia. What he does, he's a car dropper. He unloads the cars that come out of the mine."

"That don't bother my dad," the other boy said. "He likes the weather in there. It's always nice and cool. And the pay is good. It's better, anyway. The mines aren't like they used to be, I guess—the conditions. They're safer, anyway."

"My dad says things are a whole lot better," the first boy said. "And cleaner, too. He says the company used to dump the water from the coal washers in the river, but now they can't. The state won't let them. He says when he was a boy they used to dive in the river at a swimming hole they had, and he'd come up through like a foot of solid coal dust."

"I might go into the mines," the other boy said. "That's the only thing that would ever keep me here. I don't know. But the pay is good. And I kind of like these mountains. I sure don't like it where it's flat. I was up at my cousin's for a while last summer in Delaware, and it really made me feel funny. It was so flat. The only trouble here is there isn't nothing to do. There isn't no place you can go with a girl and park. Where you can be alone. What you have to do is go all the way out to the movie at Kimball—to the drive-in."

"That costs money," the first boy said.

"That's what I mean," the other boy said.

"Yeah," the first boy said. He turned back to me. "Well, thanks a lot. You can let us out at the store up there."

The store was an unpainted shed in a roadside niche in the mountain wall. The only window was broken, and there was a padlock hanging open on the door. Above the door was a homemade sign: "No Lawn Mowers Repaired Here." But the store wasn't where they were going. I watched them walk around the car and across to a little spit of land on the other side of the road. It was just big enough to accommodate a nosed-in car, and there was a drop all around of twenty feet or more to the river bottom below. At the end of the spit, a couple of feet from the edge, stood a ten-foot post with a plywood backboard at the top and a rusty basketball ring.

Photographs by David Plowden

Introduction

Berton Roueché and I have been chipping away at the same block of marble, but with different tools. As a photographer, my impressions of the desert, plains, mountains and the river are clouded by human distinctions that do not exist in nature. As environments, the differences between the desert and the plains, for example, are often determined by the fluctuation of a few inches of rainfall one way or the other. The term, "Great American Desert," which appears so frequently in the lexicon of the nineteenth-century cartographers, covered a good portion of what is "out West" to most Easterners. In dry years, the plains do become a desert—a fact which generations of homesteaders found out the hard way. But the fault was not Mother Nature's alone. Man himself, armed with plow and insatiable appetite for beef, had his share in the making of the "Great American Desert." Once laid bare by the plow, the land devoid of its ancient armor, the sod, began to be blown away by the plains' only reliable constant—the wind. And much of the rest of the uncultivated grasslands was overgrazed and trampled into a wasteland. Thus, what is really the plains and what is truly the desert is not as easy to discern as the words would have us believe.

The same is true of the land east of that imaginary delineator between the traditional prairie and the great plains, the 100th meridian. It is again a matter of more rain (and different soil) that separates them and makes the eastern land the better place for growing corn. But to the casual observer, all that vast space seems the same—

a flat and empty land, the kind of countryside that most of us on either coast tend to hurry across on our way to somewhere else.

There are obvious regional differences—the corn fields of Missouri, for example, do not look like the greasewood and sage deserts of Montana and Wyoming or Idaho. Yet, there are more similarities than differences to be found in our vast rural hinterlands. The Palouse wheat country of eastern Washington looks much like a transplanted piece of North Dakota. At first glance, most of us would be hard pressed to say whether we're in Kansas or the Dakotas or even eastern Colorado. Even what might be considered an unmistakable desert on a map is not always such to the observer. Take the Snake River Plain which, in its natural state, was one of the most inhospitable deserts North America possessed until irrigation turned parts of it into a productive garden. The desert blooms after the rain, and when the rain is supplied by sprinklers and the constant flow of water provided by a network of ditches, the results are prodigious: miles of row crops, soy beans and sugar beets, and orchards of peaches and apples and citrus groves. So long as the water pours—and man continues to enrich the land with nutrients—certain deserts become arable, even lush.

There was little "classic" desert landscape in America before man. The Mojave, the Sonoran, and Utah's Great Salt Flats come closest, and much of the West's semi-arid land has been reclaimed—if only on the most temporary basis when measured against nature's inexorable ability to reassert itself. And man's mark has likewise changed the plains and much of our other scenery. Thus, desert and plain as terms, at least visually, are often quite indistinguishable: their intrinsic natures have often been obliterated by the uses we have put them to.

Mountains, on first thought, would seem to be the most durable and easily defined of places. But the mountains in this book are not dramatic landscapes like the Rockies or the Sierra Nevadas. Here the mountains are the harsh reality of the south-central Appalachians, a beleaguered landscape synonymous with abuse and poverty. The Appalachian landscape of West Virginia reflects human despair, a despair made more eloquent by the nearby beauty of the Cumberlands, the Blue Ridge, and the glorious Smokies. Appalachia is a land of paradox: rich because it is underlain by the coal that has fired the furnaces of American industry; poor because the mining of it has exacted a toll devastating to body and land alike. To the people who live there in towns strung out along the hollows and runs and the valleys of the now blackened rivers, the mountains seem more a barrier than a source of inspiration—the walls of a prison shutting them off in a regional isolation.

There are other great rivers in America but *the* River, of course, is the Mississippi—the system through which most of the water in mid-America eventually finds its way to the sea. It has spawned a unique breed of men and boats and has produced a culture and folklore all its own. Generations of rivermen have been borne along its courses and into our minds through the pages of Francis Parkman and Mark Twain and the images of Bingham. Despite the efforts of the Corps of Engineers to transform the river into a watery interstate highway system, equipped with radar and depth indicators, it is still a place where the decisions of men and the eye of the pilot prevail. The river is its own world, unknown to those who simply cross it or traverse the "Great River Road" along its banks. Unlike Berton Roueché, I took my own trip on a large towboat up the Mississippi, instead of down.

My photographs come from many odysseys along the "blue" roads: the America of small towns, wheat fields, river worlds, and obscure crossroads—the overlooked places.

My view of the plains and deserts comes from many trips in a dozen states; the images that kindled my imagination in Idaho, for example, were somewhat different from those that inspired Mr. Roueché.

The quintessence of Appalachia I could not find in one place as my collaborator had. Besides, my collaborator had already discovered so much and described it so beautifully that there was nothing more for me to add, so I went elsewhere and came back with my own impressions, which—as always—are only fragments of what is there.

December 1974

David Plowden

Desert

Plain

the Mountains

the River